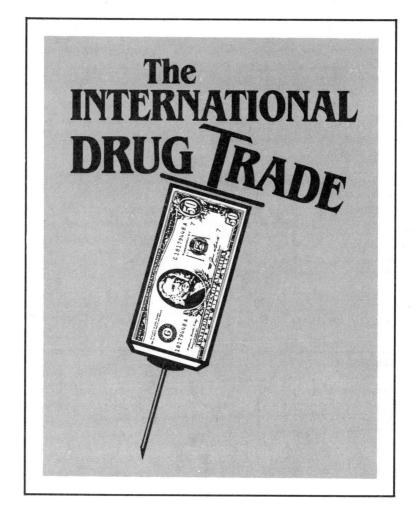

The INTERNATIONAL DRUG TRADE

Gary E. McCuen

IDEAS IN CONFLICT SERIES

publications inc.

502 Second Street
Hudson, Wisconsin 54016
Phone (715) 386-7113

18559625

$11.49

Library of Congress Cataloging-in-Publication Data

McCuen, Gary E.
    The international drug trade.

    (Ideas in conflict)
    Bibliography: p.
    1. Drug traffic. 2. Narcotics, Control of. I. Title. II. Series: Ideas in conflict series.
HV5801.M34 1989   363.4'5   88-62174
ISBN 0-86596-071-2

Illustration & photo credits

Daily World 40, 73, Jerry Fearing 83, Doug MacGregor 95, Craig MacIntosh 90, Doug Marlette 61, David Seavey 32, 66, 79, 108, 118, 123, 134, 139, 144, Carol Simpson 101, *Star Tribune* 52, United States Department of Justice 12, 114, Richard Wright 70, 129.

GEM
publications inc.
© 1989 by Gary E. McCuen Publications, Inc.
502 Second Street • Hudson, Wisconsin 54016
(715) 386-7113
International Standard Book Number 0-86596-071-2
Printed in the United States of America

CONTENTS

CHAPTER 4 CONTROLLING THE DRUG EPIDEMIC

REASONING SKILL DEVELOPMENT

These activities may be used as individualized study guides for students in libraries and resource centers or as discussion catalysts in small group and classroom discussions.

IDEAS in CONFLICT ®

This series features ideas in conflict on political, social, and moral issues. It presents counterpoints, debates, opinions, commentary, and analysis for use in libraries and classrooms. Each title in the series uses one or more of the following basic elements:

Introductions that present an issue overview giving historic background and/or a description of the controversy.

Counterpoints and debates carefully chosen from publications, books, and position papers on the political right and left to help librarians and teachers respond to requests that treatment of public issues be fair and balanced.

Symposiums and forums that go beyond debates that can polarize and oversimplify. These present commentary from across the political spectrum that reflect how complex issues attract many shades of opinion.

A *global* emphasis with foreign perspectives and surveys on various moral questions and political issues that will help readers to place subject matter in a less culture-bound and ethnocentric frame of reference. In an ever-shrinking and interdependent world, understanding and cooperation are essential. Many issues are global in nature and can be effectively dealt with only by common efforts and international understanding.

Reasoning skill study guides and discussion activities provide ready-made tools for helping with critical reading and evaluation of content. The guides and activities deal with one or more of the following:

RECOGNIZING AUTHOR'S POINT OF VIEW

INTERPRETING EDITORIAL CARTOONS

VALUES IN CONFLICT

WHAT IS EDITORIAL BIAS?

WHAT IS SEX BIAS?

WHAT IS POLITICAL BIAS?

WHAT IS ETHNOCENTRIC BIAS?

WHAT IS RACE BIAS?

WHAT IS RELIGIOUS BIAS?

*From across **the political spectrum** varied sources are presented for research projects and classroom discussions. Diverse opinions in the series come from magazines, newspapers, syndicated columnists, books, political speeches, foreign nations, and position papers by corporations and nonprofit institutions.*

About the Editor

Gary E. McCuen is an editor and publisher of anthologies for public libraries and curriculum materials for schools. Over the past 18 years his publications of over 200 titles have specialized in social, moral, and political conflict. They include books, pamphlets, cassettes, tabloids, filmstrips, and simulation games, many of them designed from his curriculums during 11 years of teaching junior and senior high school social studies. At present he is the editor and publisher of the *Ideas in Conflict* series and the *Editorial Forum* series.

CHAPTER 1

THE INTERNATIONAL DRUG TRADE: AN OVERVIEW

1.   THE WORLD'S BIGGEST BUSINESS
     J. Martinez Vera

THE INTERNATIONAL DRUG TRADE

THE WORLD'S BIGGEST BUSINESS

J. Martinez Vera

The following article was reprinted in World Press Review *(formerly* Atlas*), a magazine composed of material excerpted from the press outside the U.S.* World Press Review *is published as a nonprofit educational service to foster the international exchange of information. This article originally appeared in the newsmagazine* Cambio 16 *of Madrid.*

Points to Consider:

1. Why is the drug trade described as the world's biggest business?
2. What percentage of drug profits goes to producer countries? What happens to the rest of the money?
3. Describe the "marriage between drugs and politics." How have political leaders become involved in the drug trade? Which countries launder drug money? How are drugs and arms linked together?
4. Summarize the various ways to curb drug production and drug consumption.

J. Martinez Vera, "Supplying the 40 Million Who Won't Say No," *World Press Review,* May 1988, pp. 26-28. Reprinted with permission from the No. 849 issue of *Cambio 16.*

There are countries that would simply collapse if the drug business were to disappear overnight.

The drug trade, with a volume of $300 billion a year, is the world's biggest business. Lured by high profits, traffickers have tried to smuggle heroin in false-bottomed suitcases and in diapers. A group of Peruvians tried to smuggle a bottle of heroin-spiked shampoo through the Barcelona airport. Travelers have been detained with drugs hidden in the soles of their shoes, in beer cans, and in coffins.

There is virtually no trick that the illegal drug network has not tried to transport its wares. Two years ago, carrier pigeons were discovered flying between Venezuela and some Caribbean islands to announce the arrival of cocaine shipments.

An Army of Drug Carriers

An army of drug carriers, anti-heroes of a latter-day epic, have the job of supplying some 40 million illegal drug users throughout the world. They and their network of growers, refiners, financiers, hired killers, wholesale exporters, and retail distributors exist because users exist. Or do consumers exist because drug dealers exist? In other words, which came first—the demand for drugs, or the supply?

Answering the question would take us a long way toward resolving the problem of narcotics. There lies the crux of the serious tensions that have arisen between drug-producing and drug-consuming countries. Some, like the U.S., believe that the greatest effort should be focused on destroying drug crops and distribution channels. Others believe that so long as there is an affluent market calling for drugs, supply organizations will inevitably appear—especially if the supply comes from poorer countries that increasingly bear the burden of foreign debt and of low prices for their commodities on the world market. Obviously, there are no reliable statistics on the number of families living off the drug trade, but the people in Asia, Africa, and the Americas who depend on the poppy, coca, and cannabis crops for their livelihood number in the millions. There are countries that would simply collapse if the drug business were to disappear overnight.

The greatest financial benefits from illegal drug profits go not to the producer countries but to the consumers. The Institute for Latin American Studies at the University of St. Gallen in Switzerland estimates that barely 10 to 20 percent of all profits from drug sales go to the producer countries. Another 10 percent is funneled back into the trafficking network by way of reinvestment in laboratories, vehicles, and weapons, the experts say. The remainder winds up in the consumer countries and in the tax shelters of the world banking system.

A Drug Consumption Shopping Center

The U.S. is the drug consumption shopping center. The U.S. National Narcotics Intelligence Committee reports that in 1985 there were more than 18 million users of cannabis derivatives (marijuana and hashish) in the U.S., and 4.2 million cocaine users. By 1986, the report continues, the number of cocaine users had increased to 5.8 million (3 percent of the population), and the number of marijuana smokers had declined. Heroin is less widespread than are other drugs in the U.S., but there are some 700,000 heroin addicts.

Figures on addiction in Western Europe are few and far between, but it is estimated that there are some 1.5 million heroin users in the Common Market countries. In 1986 the European Parliament referred to heroin use as a "major epidemic" and warned, "The recent illegal consumption of drugs in the countries of the European Community is creating a complex set of problems."

Nor have the socialist countries—which until recently boasted of immunity to such decadent habits as drug abuse—been spared. In 1986, the Soviet Union's Ministry of Health publicly accepted as an ugly reality what had previously been only rumored or feared: "Drug addiction has made its appearance among us." The government acknowledged that it had 46,000 drug addicts on file.

Unlike Western European countries, which import most of their drugs, the Soviet Union produces virtually all the drugs it consumes. The Kirghiz Republic exports *koknar* (opium), *anashi* (marijuana), and hashish to other regions of the country. A government anti-drug agency has razed cannabis fields in the Valley of Chuskaya and poppy fields in the Turkmen Republic. In 1986, 300 traffickers and 4,000 retail dealers were arrested. Disturbing problems of drug addiction have emerged

11

in Stavropol, Soviet leader Mikhail Gorbachev's home ground, and in Odessa, where the weekly *Ogonyok* reports that half the addicts are teen-agers.

In Poland, one in four young people has tried drugs at least occasionally, and there are 300,000 to 600,000 habitual users of hard drugs, mainly heroin. A churchman, Father Boguslaw Bijak, calls drug addiction "a more serious problem among the young than alcoholism."

In Hungary, there are reportedly some 30,000 drug users. And Yugoslavia, which is a corridor for drugs smuggled from the Middle East and the Far East, is beginning to have its share of heroin and hashish addicts.

The problem has taken on such dimensions that the old pattern of poor producer countries and rich consumer countries no longer applies. Today there are countries that produce part of what they consume—such as the U.S., which produces 18 percent of the marijuana it smokes (compared with an insignificant share 10 years ago).

Some producer countries are beginning to experience significant levels of addiction—addiction to the poor-quality drugs that almost always fall to the poor. But the main role played by the poor countries is to supply, not to consume, drugs. In some cases, as with coca in the Andean countries or with marijuana among certain religious sects in the East Indies, drugs are part of an age-old culture.

Drugs and Politics

A recent drug phenomenon is trafficking as a political instrument. In the past few years, nearly two dozen countries have been mixed up in problems of drugs and politics. Some governments finance their armies with drug profits, but governments are not the only culprits. From the Middle East come recurrent reports that virtually all of the factions have a foothold in the heroin traffic.

Nor have European countries escaped contagion. Mauricio Coletti, head of the Italian Communist Party's anti-drug campaign, said four years ago that "drug trafficking in Italy has become a political affair that threatens democracy and is linked to every shady movement in Italian politics."

Did he exaggerate? Is the prosecutor in Miami exaggerating when he links Cuban President Fidel Castro with drug dealers, or claims that Panama's military leader, Gen. Manuel Noriega, has made $4.6 million from drug sales?

The list of countries connected with the drug trade through some political link may be as long as the list of countries that consume or produce narcotics. If we add to these the list of countries that provide a safe harbor for "hot" money, we will soon need a calculator. That list would include countries from faraway Singapore to prudent Switzerland. They—as well as Panama, the Bahamas, Hong Kong, Australia, and others—harbor and launder drug money.

A Universal Business

Drugs have become a universal business. And in general, cocaine flows north while arms flow south. The trade seems to be fairly logical.

In Colombia, where cocaine is the major export product (more than $4 billion a year), there is enough money afloat to lend credence to anybody's version of the facts: that the drug traffickers are allied with the guerrillas against the Colombian army, or that they are allied with the army to fight the guerrillas. In fact, both versions appear to be true. In some areas of the country, the cocaine growers and traffickers side with the guerrillas; in others, they side with the army.

Similarly, in Peru, which borders Colombia along a vast expanse of jungle, the police claim that the Maoist guerrilla organization "Shining Path" has a mutual-aid relationship with drug traffickers. Links between politics and the drug trade emerge in many places, but Latin America and the Caribbean head this dubious honor roll.

As political leaders become drug dealers, we should not be surprised to see some drug dealers trying to become political leaders. Pablo Escobar, a Colombian drug baron listed by *Fortune* magazine as a probable billionaire, got himself elected to Colombia's House of Representatives. In May 1984, when the Colombian government hardened its line against the drug trade following the murder of Justice Minister Rodrigo Lara Bonella, Escobar disappeared from the political scene.

The marriage between politics and drugs—occurring sometimes out of convenience and sometimes out of fear—constitutes one of the greatest threats to internal stability in some countries. This is true not only in the Third World, where countries such as Colombia have been driven to the brink of the collapse of government, but also in Europe.

As in many other countries, European governments do not realize the destabilizing power of drugs. When the Italian Communist Party warned four years ago that drugs represented "a grave danger to the democratic stability in Europe," it was clearly playing the unpopular role of prophet.

Controlling a Phantom

What can be done to control a phantom that is stalking the entire world? It is far from certain that any solution exists. Repression? Legalization? Prevention? Tough penalties? Each of these avenues has its champions, but no one has yet offered a definitive remedy.

Curbing production is a frequent recommendation. In Mexico and Colombia, chemical destruction of marijuana and coca crops has been tried. But when this remedy reduced marijuana production in Mexico, it increased production in Colombia. And when the cannabis fields in Colombia were sprayed, the Mexican share again increased, and U.S.-grown marijuana doubled. When one cartel is shut down, the others rush in to scoop up its customers.

Some advocates of curbing production believe that the wisest course is to back up crop substitution programs with economic support from the consumer countries. But the problem will remain one of supply and demand. On the day that a pound of bananas is worth more than a pound of cocaine, there will be no South American coca farmers.

Curbing consumption is another proposed remedy. The trend in many countries seems to be to treat drug use as a minor misdemeanor that may go unpunished, and to increase penalties for dealers at all levels—including those who solicit sales. Twenty-three countries have laws that impose the death penalty for drug trafficking, although only six of them have carried out executions. Malaysia is the nation with the most severe anti-drug measures. Possession of more than 200 grams of marijuana, 15 grams of heroin, or 1,000 grams of opium leads automatically and irrevocably to execution.

However, merely making the sentences harsher usually is not a sufficient deterrent. In countries with lax judicial or police institutions, this probably translates into higher bribery costs. In Malaysia in 1979, when the death penalty was at the judge's discretion in drug-trafficking cases, there were 79,000 heroin addicts. In 1986 the figure had risen to 110,000, despite the fact that hanging had become the mandatory penalty a year earlier.

Legalization of drugs is another possible remedy. The Netherlands, which had 50,000 heroin addicts in 1984, was the first country to legalize drug use. From 1977 to 1979, intravenous heroin use was permitted. But in 1980, robberies and holdups committed by drug addicts continued to increase, so the government decided to supply drugs at specialized centers to those who needed them. As a result, Holland was soon flooded with foreign junkies flocking to this paradise, and traffickers used the centers to stock up on drugs for export.

The Dutch experiment, criticized by Holland's neighbors, showed that legalizing narcotics in a few countries is no solution. More and more voices are calling for the universal legalization of drugs—putting drugs on a par with alcohol and tobacco. Advocates question whether it might not be wise to supply drugs free to addicts in order to eliminate the violence involved in supply through underworld middlemen.

Opponents of universal drug legalization believe that this measure might reduce crime rates but would not resolve the human problems of the addict. Enrique Abad, a prosecutor in Spain's drug enforcement agency, says, "We must protect public health, and we cannot accept as legal something that destroys the individual."

Controlling drug-trafficking profits is another approach. One of the few points on which there seems to be an international consensus is the need to monitor the money generated by drug trafficking. That was the main conclusion reached in Vienna at the First International Conference Against Drugs in 1987. Several European countries are considering measures that will hurt traffickers' pocketbooks. A drug law recently enacted in Spain provides for confiscating assets acquired through drug trafficking—including property acquired with laundered money.

These measures may help, but none is a panacea for this spreading ill. Some experts believe that governments could eradicate drugs if they were determined to do so, but that, for political reasons, they do not want them to disappear. Others say that a change in economic structures might solve the drug problem—that a solution lies in a new society that does not need drugs.

EXAMINING COUNTERPOINTS

This activity may be used as an individualized study guide for students in libraries and resource centers or as a discussion catalyst in small group and classroom discussions.

The Point

Illegal drugs are not a growing problem in America. This country's biggest problems are alcohol and tobacco, the social costs of which dwarf those of all illicit drugs combined. Yet they remain legal, cheap and even subsidized, in the case of tobacco, with tax dollars.

The Counterpoint

Illegal drugs are a widespread problem in America. Although alcohol and tobacco abuse is also a problem, illicit drugs are rapidly becoming a growing tragedy in this country, affecting poor and affluent communities alike. Illegal drugs threaten to affect everyone—medically, financially, and in terms of productivity.

Guidelines

Part A

Examine the counterpoints above and then consider the following questions.

1. Do you agree more with the point or counterpoint? Why?

2. Which reading in this book best illustrates the point?

3. Which reading best illustrates the counterpoint?

4. Do any cartoons in this book illustrate the meaning of the point or counterpoint arguments? Which ones and why?

Part B

Social issues are usually complex, but often problems become over-simplified in political debates and discussions. Usually a polarized version of social conflict does not adequately represent the diversity of views that surround social conflicts. Examine the counterpoints. Then write down possible interpretations of this issue other than the two arguments stated in the counterpoints.

CHAPTER 2

BUCKS FOR BANKERS:
WASHING DIRTY MONEY

2 BUCKS FOR BANKERS: WASHING DIRTY MONEY

HOW MONEY IS LAUNDERED: AN OVERVIEW

U.S. Department of State

The Department of State's International Narcotics Control Strategy Report (INCSR) is prepared in accordance with the provisions of Section 481 of the Foreign Assistance Act of 1961, as amended (22 U.S.C. 2291). The 1988 INCSR is the second annual report prepared pursuant to Section 2005 of P.L. 99-570, the Anti-Drug Abuse Act of 1986. The Bureau of International Narcotics Matters of the U.S. Department of State presented the INCSR on March 1, 1988, to the Committee on Foreign Affairs and the Committee of Foreign Relations.

Points to Consider:

1. How is drug money laundered?
2. What are the effects of money laundering?
3. Describe the enforcement activities that have been undertaken in the past several years against money launderers and financial institutions.
4. Why are some governments reluctant to cooperate with the U.S. anti-money laundering program?

United States Department of State (Bureau of International Narcotics Matters), *International Narcotics Control Strategy Report* (Washington, D.C.: March 1988), pp. 43-51.

While some governments have been sincere in trying to deal with these issues, an important number have not yet taken meaningful action to prevent narcotics money laundering.

Money Laundering

While significant actions against money laundering were taken in 1987, the foreign policy and enforcement communities agree that much more action needs to be taken by all affected governments to curb narcotics money laundering. This overview reports on U.S. activities to increase the investigation and suppression of narcotics money laundering, and importantly, to curb narcotics money flows.

It is important to understand that money laundering is a vital component of drug trafficking operations throughout the world; laundering schemes do not merely provide the conduits for financing narcotics ventures, they also conceal the true nature or source of narcodollars and disguise those funds to make them appear legitimate. Thus, tracing and seizing and otherwise interrupting the flow of narcodollars is an important part of the overall effort to disrupt narcotics production and trafficking. There is still no definitive answer to such questions as: What happens to all of the profits generated by illicit narcotics production and trafficking? There is an answer of many parts: some profits are used to sustain trafficker networks and operations; the larger shares are used for various licit and illicit investments, or to indulge luxurious life-styles, or to support political insurgencies, or to pay off corrupt officials and politicians, or to finance other kinds of illicit criminal activity. . . .

This report employs the terms of reference contained in the Money Laundering Control Act of 1986, which became Subtitle H of Title I of P.L. 99-570. Money laundering occurs whenever a person, knowing that the property involved in a financial transaction represents the proceeds of some form of unlawful activity (e.g., narcotics trafficking), conducts or attempts to conduct such a financial transaction which in fact involves the proceeds of specified unlawful activity (a) with the intent to promote the carrying on of specified unlawful activity, or (b) knowing that the transaction is designed in whole or in part to conceal or disguise the nature, the location, the source, the ownership, or the control of the proceeds of specified unlawful activity, or to avoid a transaction reporting requirement. The offense of money laundering also occurs with respect to the transporting of monetary instruments or funds with the intent to carry on a specified unlawful activity, or when the person knows that the instruments or funds represent the proceeds of some form of unlawful activity, and knows the transport is designed to con-

THE BANK OF BOSTON CASE

The Bank of Boston case drew bankers' attention to the cash reporting law. Since then, the number of transactions reported to the federal government has doubled. More than 40 other banks nationwide have informed the Treasury Department that they too had accepted millions of dollars in cash without reporting the transactions. They include Shawmut and Bank of New England.

Bank of Boston's audit department reviewed its compliance with the law in 1977. Although it identified only one transaction where the bank failed to file a report, deputy auditor Perley A. Swasey Jr. sounded an ominous note.

"The prevalent weakness. . . was that tellers and teller trainees at the branches we reviewed had not been informed of Operational Procedure. . . . Although Branch Management was aware of the Bank Secrecy Act, and possessed written procedures in the new Retail Banking Operating Manual, it appears that tellers weren't aware of proper procedures."

Excerpted from a Boston Globe *Spotlight Team report on money laundering, 1985.*

ceal the nature, location, source of ownership, or control of such instruments or funds.

A "transaction" includes a purchase, sale, loan, pledge, gift, transfer, delivery, or other disposition. With respect to a financial institution, it means a deposit, withdrawal, transfer between accounts, exchange of currency, loan, extension of credit, purchase or sale of any stock, bond, certificate of deposit, or any other payment, transfer or delivery by, through, or to a financial institution.

How Money Is Laundered

Cash is the medium of exchange in the world of drugs, and "drug money laundering" is the process of changing the money gained from narcotics operations from cash into a more manageable form of cash or other form of proceeds while concealing its illicit origins. Typically, the process involves use of foreign bank accounts and a series of intermediate shelters for money, such as dummy corporations set up to offer plausible explanations for money and to confuse investigators. Many techniques for laundering drug money were developed by other businesses to evade taxes, but because of the large amounts of cash and the special risks that accompany the movement of drug money, the narcotics trafficker's laundering needs are unusual.

MONEY LAUNDERING

Drug traffickers prefer a climate of political stability: regulations that assure a degree of bank secrecy; little or no tax liability; if possible, systems where large scale bribery and corruption may be available options; and a financial system sophisticated enough to handle large transactions efficiently. Historically, money laundering centers have developed where some combination of these characteristics exists, as in Panama, the Bahamas, the Cayman Islands, Switzerland, and the Channel Islands, rather than in solely drug producing nations.

Narcodollar laundering operations are usually isolated from production and trafficking activities, not only because of the enforcement pressures cited above, but also because of their differing financial requirements and traffickers' desire to keep these operations compartmented.

The Caribbean Basin is the first stop for most Latin American drug dollars moving through international channels. For both the foreign suppliers and their U.S. distributors, the Caribbean Basin has long been a natural stop because of its proximity to the United States, high levels of corruption, and the region's many financial centers with secrecy laws and lenient taxes. Most of the rest of the laundered funds, mainly relating to heroin trafficking, go to Western Europe and Hong Kong.

In some European countries, bank secrecy is a product of history and strongly held beliefs concerning individual privacy and the sanctity of contracts. It is, therefore, important to bear in mind whenever discussing a country with strict banking secrecy laws that, in most instances, those laws do not exist for the purpose of facilitating money laundering or of hiding the sources of funds.

Drug money moves into international channels in four basic ways:

(1) Large amounts of U.S. currency—estimated in billions of dollars annually—are physically moved out of the United States and deposited in financial institutions abroad. Drug traders using this method must deal with the problem of bulky shipments moved under risky conditions and with U.S. reporting requirements for cash movements exceeding $10,000.

(2) To avoid the need to handle bulk amounts of cash, drug money launderers frequently deposit currency into bank accounts in the United States and then request the bank to wire funds to an account abroad. Major risks for traffickers include the paper trail that is created by currency transactions of more than $10,000 and by wire transfers. Launderers can reduce these risks by blending drug-related money with legal funds before depositing the cash in a bank. Thus, by the time the money is transferred abroad, its illegal source has been concealed.

(3) Carrying financial instruments abroad has an advantage over moving currency because of the smaller bulk involved. Some types of financial paper (e.g., bearer bonds and cashier's checks) are not made out to an individual, and like cash, leave a minimal paper trail.

(4) Drug traffickers can launder their funds through non-financial movements that resemble legitimate transactions. For example, money launderers can buy goods such as autos or appliances in the United States for cash and ship them abroad to be sold for local currency. With help from an accomplice abroad, money launderers can also use a technique called "over invoicing," i.e., buying goods abroad at much higher than market prices. When traffickers pay for these goods out of their U.S. bank accounts, the drug money has moved home.

Once funds are abroad, they are usually moved several times through secret bank accounts, trusts, or shell corporations and can cross several international boundaries. These movements are intended to blur further the distinction between illicit drug money and the billions of legitimate dollars that move through the international financial system every day. Some funds are also used to pay drug suppliers and others who provide services to narcotics operations.

There are no accurate figures on the amount of money generated from drug transactions which is returned and spent in the United States. One avenue for the return of drug proceeds to the United States is through sham loans from foreign to domestic corporations. Drug traffickers move money out of the United States into foreign shell corporations and then arrange for business loans to domestic shell corporations. This allows the drug traffickers to gain access to the drug money in the United States as well as creating bogus tax deductions based on interest paid on the loan. Some drug money launderers have engaged in large-scale real estate development through foreign shell corporations.

The techniques of money laundering are innumerable, diverse, complex, subtle, and secret. While billions of drug dollars are laundered annually, the exact amount remains unknown and is a fraction of the world's fast-moving international financial activity, a fact that drug traffickers and launderers rely on to obscure their activities. Only by tracking the origin and destination of each transaction is there a reasonable expectation that its narcotics-derived source can be discovered.

Effects of Money Laundering

From different vantage points, there are both positive and negative perceptions of the effects of narcotics money laundering. Proceeds from drug trafficking are used to finance other criminal activities, to undermine legitimate businesses, to threaten governments, to corrupt public institutions and officials, and support insurgencies. Illicit profits drive up real estate costs, and otherwise manipulate regular commerce.

Despite these serious problems, laundering criminally derived money can provide benefits to some otherwise economically unattractive countries. Such monies create an influx of capital which can lead to a stimulation of the country's economy. The increase in capital created by the criminally derived money increases money reserves, lowers interest rates, creates new jobs and, in general, encourages economic activity. Some officials are, therefore, reluctant to take action or provide information on money laundering activities.

The Anti-Money Laundering Program

Diplomatic Activities

U.S. and international anti-narcotics policymakers and enforcement officers are strongly committed to sustaining and improving an effective global strategy that includes eradication of illicit crops, suppression of manufacturing and refining facilities, seizures of drugs and contraband, monitoring of shipments of precursor chemicals, and arrest and prosecution of traffickers and money launderers. Today, there is a realization that, while traditional narcotics enforcement activities must be expanded and enhanced, new techniques and methods must be developed to apprehend major traffickers and financiers and destabilize their criminal networks. Similarly, more must be done to prevent the profits of illicit narcotics transactions from becoming a dependent part of local and national economies, from undermining legitimate commerce and industry, and from sustaining political insurgents and terrorists.

Beyond seizing shipments of illicit drugs, U.S. officials are therefore seeking greater cooperation from foreign counterparts on seizure and forfeiture of trafficker assets, with a special focus on tracing and seizing the monetary assets derived from narcotics trafficking. Such investigations and seizures have a dual benefit: they reduce the operating capacity of drug networks, and they can lead to prosecution of major traffickers. . . .

Enforcement Activities

The law enforcement community considers money laundering a vital component of a well-organized drug trafficking operation, and federal and state agencies have begun to focus resources on attacking the financial aspects of drug organizations. Several enforcement initiatives have been undertaken in the past several years against money launderers and financial institutions. The following examples are illustrative.

Operation Cashweb/Expressway was a three-year undercover operation which penetrated the highest levels of three money laundering organizations of Colombian drug-trafficking syndicates operating in South America and the United States. During this investigation, FBI undercover agents laundered millions of dollars in order to reveal conspiratorial networks. Agents identified over $300 million in Colombian drug proceeds. Thus far, this case has achieved the following results: Federal, state, and local indictments of 114 conspirators for drug and/or money laundering violations; the seizure of 2,100 pounds of cocaine, 22,000 pounds of marijuana and $22.5 million in cash. Additionally, $11 million has been identified in bank accounts of two major subjects and forfeiture proceedings have been initiated against these accounts.

From 1982 to 1987, the FBI directed an international investigation focused on heroin importation and distribution and money laundering by Sicilian Mafia figures in association with the La Cosa Nostra in the

United States. This historic investigation was commonly referred to by the media as the "Pizza Connection" case, because the Mafia used pizza parlors throughout New York and five other states to facilitate the distribution of an estimated $1.65 billion worth of heroin smuggled into this country from Sicily. The FBI, with support from the Drug Enforcement Administration (DEA), the U.S. Customs Service and foreign governments, as well as numerous state and local law enforcement agencies, revealed the scheme in which morphine base was transported from Turkey for conversion to heroin in clandestine laboratories in Sicily. This investigation resulted in the indictment of 38 high-level traffickers in the U.S. and an additional 175 Mafia members and associates in Italy for drug trafficking and money laundering violations. Trial testimony and evidence gathered during the investigation revealed that this drug group had laundered approximately $60 million in heroin-trafficking proceeds through legitimate businesses in the United States and abroad. In 1987, 18 defendants, including Gaetano Badalamenti, the former Sicilian Mafia "Boss of All Bosses," were sentenced in federal court in New York to jail terms up to 45 years. . . .

For years, financial institutions have been utilized to launder illicit drug profits. To curtail this activity, Congress enacted the 1970 Bank Secrecy Act which requires financial institutions to report currency transactions in excess of $10,000. However, banks and bankers alike have fallen victim (willing and unwilling) to huge profits which result from laundering activities. A federal grand jury indicted the Great American Bank of Dade County, Florida, and three employees. The indictments, returned as a series from December 1982 through April 1984, charged that the bank laundered more than $94 million from January 1980 through February 1981, and willfully failed to file 406 currency transaction reports (CTR's) during that period. On April 16, 1984, the bank pled guilty to four counts of failure to file CTR's and was fined $500,000.

The publicity in February 1985 regarding the conviction of the Bank of Boston in a money laundering scheme has quadrupled the reporting of currency transactions. From 1985 to the present, nearly three dozen institutions have been penalized. The Treasury Department levied heavy fines in 1985 and 1986 on several financial institutions for violations of Bank Secrecy Act reporting requirements. Treasury investigators discovered that Crocker National Bank failed to report $3.4 billion of domestic and international cash deposits and withdrawals. In September, Treasury assessed a fine of $2.25 million on the bank. In January 1986, Bank of America was fined $4.75 million for failure to report more than 17,000 cash transactions.

Until the enactment of the Money Laundering Control Act of 1986, money laundering was not considered a felony in and of itself. However, several major initiatives against individuals and institutions were concluded with positive results. It is believed that with the new legislation and experience gained in financial investigations, positive results will only increase.

Challenges and Problems

Research and intelligence gathering relating to the operation of money launderers, their methods and schemes is still in its infancy. Although it has been recognized for some years that a collateral attack on the proceeds of drug trafficking is a very effective way to immobilize trafficking organizations, much remains to be done. Tracing, tracking, seizure, and forfeiture of violator assets have been increasingly successful in the United States in recent years. Undercover probes of money laundering activities and the overt collection of financial intelligence have provided important insights into the shadowy world of the money launderer.

Initial success notwithstanding, these efforts have been frustrated in several ways. Drug traffickers are as circumspect in their financial dealings as they are in their drug negotiations. The traffickers' appreciation for the need to conceal their enormous profits is increasing. This awareness, coupled with constant and complex changes in money laundering practices, has resulted in an ever-expanding and dynamic laundering system. Finally, and perhaps most importantly, many if not most money laundering schemes at some point involve the clandestine movement of assets to or through other countries. The climate for cooperation can vary sharply from country to country, even within the same region.

Given the political sensitivities and realities associated with narcotics production and trafficking in different nations, the reception given to U.S. requests for cooperation has been mixed. There is unquestionably an increasing awareness among nations that the laundering of drug proceeds must be urgently addressed. Most heads of state and diplomatic officials want to avoid having their countries become the drug money capitals of the world. Many senior foreign officials recognize that the seizure and forfeiture of drug proceeds is an effective way to frustrate traffickers and disrupt their operations. Officials have also recognized that forfeiture of large amounts of criminally derived assets can be an appreciable source of revenues.

As a result, some governments have enacted strict domestic legislation prohibiting certain types of financial activity and have mandated actions which breach traditional bank secrecy when drug money is involved. Other countries have taken further steps, either formally or informally arranging to make bank information available to U.S. authorities and, in some cases, have passed legislation which permits the seizure and forfeiture of assets based upon evidence collected almost entirely in the United States.

But, while many of these nations are willing to take energetic steps to combat an influx of drug money, a number of governments are reluctant to interfere with their status as offshore tax havens. Many governments face objections from strong bank lobbies, whose constituents stand to lose substantial deposits, commissions, and fees if their governments outlaw trafficking in drug proceeds. These legal barriers and prohibitions are just one challenge. Corruption is a problem that affects all anti-narcotics initiatives, including investigations into money laundering. Moreover, some banks are apparently controlled by or at least heavily influenced by narcotics trafficking interests. There are numerous ways a government can frustrate U.S. initiatives while appearing to be cooperative; e.g., resistance can be masked by meaningless legislative initiatives, unprogressive dialogue with the United States on cooperation, or informal cooperation on a few cases to protect broader narcodollar laundering interests.

In sum, while some governments have been sincere in trying to deal with these issues, an important number have not yet taken meaningful action to prevent narcotics money laundering.

BUCKS FOR BANKERS: WASHING DIRTY MONEY

THE BANKS ARE LAUNDERING MILLIONS

Richard C. Wassenaar

Richard C. Wassenaar presented the following testimony in his capacity as the Assistant Commissioner (Criminal Investigation) for the Internal Revenue Service (IRS). The Criminal Investigation unit investigates alleged violations of the Internal Revenue Laws and related offenses and certain aspects of the Bank Secrecy Act.

Points to Consider:

1. Summarize the Bank Secrecy Act.
2. Describe the Garfield Bank's involvement in money laundering. How much money was laundered through the Garfield Bank?
3. Who belonged to the Botero Organization? How were they involved in money laundering?
4. Why does the author advocate the need for regulating changes with regard to multiple transactions?

Excerpted from testimony of Richard C. Wassenaar before the House Subcommittee on Financial Institutions Supervision, Regulation and Insurance of the House Committee on Banking, Finance and Urban Affairs, April 16, 1986.

The international banking network offers the efficiency, security, and most of all privacy, cherished by criminals who specialize in money laundering, tax evasion, and other financial crimes.

Introduction

We at the Internal Revenue Service (IRS) believe that devoting substantial resources to the investigation of money laundering is appropriate not only because of the significant amount of revenue that can be collected, but also because the Services's tax administration expertise can be focused on the motive for drug trafficking—the huge illegal profits involved. In order to stem the flow of drugs we must attack the movement of funds generated by this illegal activity.

Money laundering is big business. It is also a business with a varied clientele: drug dealers saddled with millions of dollars in cash per week; ostensibly legitimate businessmen trying to evade taxes; giant corporations setting up slush funds for bribes and kickbacks; and ordinary people trying to hide their assets. . . .

Bank Secrecy Act

I would like to begin with a brief review of the Bank Secrecy Act in order to place our activities in perspective.

As a result of concerns expressed by law enforcement over the laundering of illegally generated proceeds through domestic banks and foreign tax havens, Congress passed the Bank Secrecy Act in 1970 (P.L. 91-508). The Act provided four basic tools to identify those who attempt to conceal their participation in crimes where substantial amounts of currency are generated, and to provide a basis to prosecute those who fail to comply with its requirements. The Act focuses on individuals involved in the *flow* of currency, as opposed to those involved in the substantive violations that *generated* the currency. Legislative history of the Act shows that Congress explicitly recognized the value of the Act to have a high degree of usefulness in criminal, tax, or regulatory investigations or proceedings.

The four basic tools provided:

- A paper trail of records that must be maintained by financial institutions for up to five years. These records include copies of checks, drafts, money orders, and customer identification information.

- A Currency Transaction Report (CTR) that must be filed by banks and other financial institutions whenever a currency transaction over $10,000 occurs.

- A Currency or Monetary Instruments Report (CMIR) whenever currency or monetary instruments over $10,000 are taken into or out of the U.S. Offenses relating to the transportation of currency across U.S. borders are investigated by U.S. Customs.

- A Foreign Bank Account Report (FBAR) is required whenever a person has a financial interest in or signature authority over a foreign financial account in excess of $10,000 in value.

In addition, recent regulatory amendments added additional reporting requirements:

Casinos with gross annual gaming revenue over $1,000,000 are added to the list of financial institutions that must file CTR's for currency transactions over $10,000.

The Secretary of the Treasury may require certain financial institutions to report transactions with foreign financial agencies. These transactions include wire transfers, checks or drafts, loans, commercial paper, stocks, bonds, and certificates of deposit.

There are both civil and criminal penalties associated with violations of the Bank Secrecy Act. Civil violations can result in penalties of up to $10,000 per violation. Criminal penalties can result in a maximum prison term of up to five years and a fine of up to $250,000.

Cartoon by David Seavey. Copyright 1985, *USA Today.* Reprinted with permission.

When the violation is committed in furtherance of the commission of any other violation of federal law, or is committed as part of a pattern of illegal activity involving transactions exceeding $100,000 in any 12-month period, then the maximum fine is increased to $500,000.

The IRS has the responsibility to conduct Bank Secrecy Act criminal investigations of all banks and other financial institutions. The IRS also conducts civil compliance examinations of secondary financial institutions. Secondary financial institutions include, but are not limited to, non-regulated banks, casinos, and currency exchange houses. . . .

Enforcement Efforts

The IRS has made substantial progress in its enforcement efforts. Since October 1981, we have initiated criminal investigations of more than 873 money laundering specialists, corrupt financial institutions, and their employees.

As of January 31, 1986, Criminal Investigation has over 300 Bank Secrecy Act investigations currently in open inventory. Over 60 of these are investigations of financial institutions. During 1985, we recommended prosecution of 317 cases involving money laundering.

We have presented evidence leading to the conviction of a total of 31 banks and financial institutions since 1981, with eight convictions in the past year alone. These banks have been criminally fined nearly $4,000,000. In addition, we have presented evidence leading to the conviction of 34 officers or employees of financial institutions since 1984.

Examples of Bank Involvement

Money laundering specialists use a number of techniques to provide services for their clients. These range from cash transported offshore in suitcases, to elaborate unofficial banking operations, to the use of fictitious offshore entities.

I would like to describe some of the cases we have investigated, which involve complicity by the financial institutions used by the launderers.

Garfield Bank

In 1981, an undercover operation in Southern California focused on the laundering of narcotics money through a Los Angeles bank with the assistance of top bank officials.

Nathan Markowitz, a Los Angeles attorney, acted as a "money laundering specialist" who provided the service of disguising the source of profits earned by his clients, who were California narcotics traffickers.

Markowitz established nominee accounts at the Garfield Bank, and sham corporations in the State of California. He also established foreign corporations in Panama and Liberia, and trusts at the Bank of Bermuda, where bank secrecy laws prevent law enforcement authorities from obtaining records. Large amounts of currency were deposited into various domestic accounts over which Markowitz maintained control. This money was then wire-transferred to trusts at the Bank of Bermuda or was used to purchase cashier's checks at the Garfield Bank for Markowitz's clients.

The key to the initial success of the laundering operation in this case was the complicity of bank officials who willingly and knowingly failed to file CTR's.

The president, and two vice-presidents, allegedly to increase the volume of business, arranged with Markowitz to accept the cash deposits of Markowitz's narcotics trafficker clients. Although each

33

deposit exceeded $10,000, CTR's were not filed. Over a two-year period, Markowitz laundered a total of $3.3 million with the assistance of these bank officials.

The three Garfield Bank officials and three of Markowitz's associates were subsequently convicted of felony violations of the Bank Secrecy Act for their involvement in the failure to file CTR's for the money that was laundered through the Garfield Bank. The Garfield Bank was also convicted of Bank Secrecy Act violations and was fined $309,106, an amount equal to their net income for 1980.

Markowitz was murdered prior to trial. Los Angeles newspaper reports speculated that the murder was motivated by Markowitz's agreement to cooperate with the government. . . .

Botero

In January 1981, several Colombian nationals (known collectively as the Botero Organization) and U.S. citizens were charged with attempting to launder $57 million in U.S. currency through the branch of the Fort Lauderdale bank in an eight-month period. It was alleged that this currency represented payments from domestic narcotics organizations to Colombian source suppliers for cocaine and marijuana smuggled into the United States and distributed through domestic trafficking organizations. The ultimate street value of the drugs would be over half a billion dollars. While this $57 million represents the wholesalers' receipts, it includes none of the profits reaped by the domestic organizations.

The Botero Organization enlisted the assistance of three bank officers at a small branch of a major Florida bank. Being paid a cash fee of 0.5 to 1.0 percent of the monies to be laundered, the officers opened numerous bank accounts in fictitious names with fictitious identification. The idea was to accept the cash deposits, run this cash through the bank accounts and file false currency transaction reports. The funds would then be wire-transferred from the numerous accounts at the primary bank to a correspondent account of a foreign bank in Miami. From this second account the funds would be wire-transferred offshore and distributed to other accounts in a foreign country. The U.S. dollars would then be available for a variety of uses, including sale on the black market for Colombian pesos or simply to secure wealth in U.S. dollar denominated instruments.

The currency deposited into this small branch bank in Fort Lauderdale was a contributing factor to the enormous surplus of currency at the Miami branch of the Federal Reserve. During the late 1970's this surplus in the amount of currency from Southern Florida financial institutions led us to believe that lucrative criminal activities were the source of these funds.

After the indictments in this case were returned, Herman Botero, a prominent Colombian businessman and owner of the national soccer team, fled the U.S. Botero became the first Colombian national ordered extradited to the United States by the Supreme Court of Colombia. He was convicted in 1985 and sentenced to serve 30 years in prison.

Although Botero and his associates were successfully prosecuted, most of the $57 million was transferred out of the country and the remainder distributed throughout the United States. We have no authority to seize and forfeit the funds. This case points to the need for legal authority to seize and forfeit currency (and property traceable to such currency) involved in CTR violations.

We have some concern that professional money launderers or narcotics traffickers may attempt to gain financial control of financial institutions to facilitate their money laundering activities. The Drug Enforcement Administration was successful in recent prosecutions of a drug ring in which the leader, Jose Antonio Fernandez, owned a controlling interest in the Sunshine State Bank in Miami, Florida.

We are alert for such situations, and are currently conducting several investigations in which individuals involved in criminal activity may have an ownership interest in a financial institution.

I do not want to leave you with the impression that all money laundering through banks and financial institutions is accomplished with the complicity of the institution. In fact, most of the schemes we investigate include money launderers who have gone to great lengths to prevent the financial institutions from being aware they are moving a large amount of currency through the institutions.

Multiple Transactions and the Need for Regulatory Change

While we have been quite successful in prosecuting banks for willful violations of the Bank Secrecy Act, we have been considerably less successful in prosecuting bank customers who deliberately prevent the institution from filing a CTR. A great concern of late in enforcing the Act is the problem of customers structuring currency transactions into increments of less than $10,000 in order to prevent the financial institution from filing a CTR. Financial institutions must file a CTR with the IRS for currency transactions over $10,000. A person who wishes to transact a large amount of currency at a financial institution for deposit into an account, wire-transfer offshore, or to purchase monetary instruments, will often hire one or more individuals (we call them "smurfs") to scurry from bank to bank with increments of less than $10,000 in order to assure that no CTR's are filed. Through these multiple transactions, the money launderer is able to defeat the purpose of the Bank Secrecy Act. We are deprived of CTR's that would be of great value in investigating and prosecuting individuals involved in illegal drug trafficking and tax crimes.

The person who engages in the multiple transactions and thereby causes the CTR not to be filed is not guilty of illegal conduct in many situations. The 1st, 9th, and 11th Circuits have recently indicated that smurfing, at least if conducted at different banks on the same day, or at the same bank on different days, is not a crime. As a result, the government needs to make the program effective. Smurfing becomes a legal way to defeat the purpose of the law, i.e., the detection of illegal activity and tax evasion. . . .

Conclusion

In the last decade traditional financial institutions have become vital, albeit often unwitting, participants in all sorts of illegal activities. The international banking network offers the efficiency, security, and most of all privacy, cherished by criminals who specialize in money laundering, tax evasion, and other financial crimes.

These criminals have learned how to make the maximum use of international banking services. Funds are wire-transferred out of the United States and then sent on a Caribbean Island hopping tour from one haven bank to another in order to cover the trail. The final foreign destination is often a traditional European financial center from which the funds can be repatriated with an added appearance of legitimacy.

Money laundering is not just a problem for law enforcement. The illicit money circulating through the financial bloodstream of our country is a poison that attacks the health of the financial community itself. The good reputation of financial institutions who are found to have laundered illicit funds can be deeply scarred in the eyes of the public even if none of the officers or employees are culpable. Moreover, we are seeing cases in which banks are actually the prey of the white collar criminal. A solution to the money laundering problem will take the joint effort of government and the financial community. We must commit ourselves to make sacrifices and pursue with vigor those who would disrupt the free flow of commerce to facilitate their corrupting criminal activities.

BUCKS FOR BANKERS:
WASHING DIRTY MONEY

BANKERS ARE COMPLYING
WITH THE LAW

Earl B. Hadlow

Earl B. Hadlow presented the following testimony in his capacity as Vice Chairman and General Counsel of Barnett Banks of Jacksonville, Florida, and as a member of the American Bankers Association Government Relations Council. Mr. Hadlow testified on behalf of the American Bankers Association.

Points to Consider:

1. Study the quotes of Mr. R. L. Wood and the General Counsel of the ABA. What is the general message of these two quotes?
2. Does the ABA support criminalizing money laundering? Why or why not?
3. Describe the proposed legislation to which Mr. Hadlow refers in his testimony. Which proposals does the ABA support and why?
4. Does the ABA support amending the Right to Financial Privacy Act? Why or why not?

Excerpted from testimony of Earl B. Hadlow before the Subcommittee on Financial Institution Supervision, Regulation, and Insurance of the House Committee on Banking, Finance and Urban Affairs, May 14, 1986.

The American Bankers Association wants to maintain a balance between the legitimate needs of law enforcement and the legitimate need to protect customers' privacy from unlimited government intrusion.

I welcome the opportunity to present the American Banking Association's (ABA) views on H.R. 1367, H.R. 1474, H.R. 1945, H.R. 2785, H.R. 3892, H.R. 4280, H.R. 4573 and Titles I, VI, and XI of the Financial Institutions Regulatory and Interest Rate Control Act of 1978.

A number of the bills that have been introduced will amend the Currency and Foreign Transaction Reporting Act (Bank Secrecy Act); severely weaken the Right to Financial Privacy Act (RFPA); and create a federal crime of money laundering.

The ABA understands the challenge that law enforcement officials face in attempting to combat drug trafficking and organized crime. The use of financial institutions as havens for drug money is as abhorrent to our members as it is to the public in general. We want to maintain a balance between the legitimate needs of law enforcement and the legitimate need to protect our customers' privacy from unlimited government intrusion.

Our feelings were best summed up by Mr. R. L. Wood when he appeared before the House Committee on Ways and Means on July 18, 1975, and said:

> The right to privacy of an individual's financial records. . . in the absence of a *known violation* of law by the individual involving his finances. . . is an integral element of the American concept of political rights of the individual. These rights have been characterized as being protected under our Constitution and under the common law.

Mr. Wood's remarks were based upon our policy as expressed by the General Counsel of the American Bankers Association in 1940, when he said:

> A bank should, as a general policy, consider information concerning its customers as confidential, which it should not disclose to others without clear justification. *Milohnich v. First National Bank of Miami Springs,* 224 So. 2d. 759, 761 (1969).

We Need Universally Acceptable Legislation

A small number of financial institutions have been fined for failure to file the reports required by the Bank Secrecy Act. In cases where employees of the financial institutions have conspired with criminal elements to evade the reporting requirements, individuals have been brought to trial by the Department of Justice. The violations of the reporting requirements have exacted a swift response by our banks. The industry has dramatically increased its educational programs and compliance efforts. The financial industry's repeated requests for practical solutions have thus far only been met by echoes of our inadvertent reporting failures. Now is the time to focus on the future, not dwell on the past.

The numerous bills now pending reflect the concerns of Congress about the problem of drug trafficking. As this Committee focuses on possible solutions to that problem, you should follow the advice of your chairman "to enact something now that is universally acceptable." Universally acceptable legislation will maintain the "proper regard for civil liberties" and will also "throw the gauntlet down against money laundering transactions."

The first step toward solving the problem is to separate out those issues that will prevent the enactment of acceptable legislation. The two proposals that we believe will prevent immediate action are a new crime of money laundering and amending the Right to Financial Privacy Act.

The ABA continues to support making money laundering a crime. However, the process of criminalizing money laundering demands broad-based discussions on its possible ramifications. The shaping of the crime must be done with a scalpel, not a shotgun. Therefore, now is not the time to tackle a new Title 18 crime.

Mutual Bank & Trust Co.

DEPOSITS
WITHDRAWALS

MORTGAGE
PAYMENTS

TRAVELER'S
CHECKS

MONEY
LAUNDERING

H. Goldberg

Various Legislative Proposals

A number of proposals repeal the procedural safeguards found in The Right to Financial Privacy Act (RFPA). We are not convinced that the procedural protections in the RFPA severely hamper law enforcement activities. Therefore, we do not believe it should be amended in any fashion.

H.R. 1367 as introduced by Representative McCollum contains many of the recommendations made in the Interim Report of the President's Commission on Organized Crime. Included in H.R. 1367 are a new crime of money laundering, changes in the federal wiretap statute, and changes in the Right to Financial Privacy Act.

H.R. 1367 would also expand the authority of the Secretary of the Treasury under the Bank Secrecy Act (BSA). The Secretary would be given the authority to examine any data or records of a domestic financial institution required by the recordkeeping requirements of BSA. In addition, the Secretary could summon an officer or employee of a financial institution to appear before the Secretary or his delegate and produce such records, data, or sworn testimony as may be relevant or material.

The bill proposes making judicial orders authorizing wiretaps for the interception of telephone calls, telexes, and other forms of wire or oral communications available for investigations of possible violations of the criminal provisions of the Bank Secrecy Act (i.e. willful violation of the reporting requirements) and of the proposed crime of money laundering.

H.R. 1474 as introduced by Representative Hughes creates a new crime of money laundering and requires individuals to file directly with the Secretary of the Treasury for exemption from the BSA reporting requirements.

H.R. 1945, as introduced by Representative Hubbard contains two titles. First, it contains the Drug Money Seizure Act, which would increase the penalties for a willful violation of the Bank Secrecy Act. As proposed, the current civil penalty of $10,000 would be increased to the amount of the transaction where the violation involved a transaction reporting requirement. This provision introduces the concept of forfeiture as a penalty. Mr. Hubbard's bill also grants the Secretary of the Treasury summons authority. This is a response to the assertion by the Department of the Treasury that it lacks subpoena power sufficient to enforce the Bank Secrecy Act. If the Congress finds that the current means of obtaining a subpoena available to the Secretary of the Treasury are inadequate to enforce the Act, we would support the expansion of the Treasury's subpoena authority as proposed. Secondly, H.R. 1945 creates a crime of money laundering.

H.R. 2785 ("the Administration bill"), as introduced by Representatives St. Germain and Wylie at the request of the Administration, creates among other things a new crime of money laundering, amends the Federal Rules of Criminal procedure, and establishes criminal and civil forfeiture under Title 18.

H.R. 2785 also gives the Secretary of the Treasury authority to examine records, papers, and other data of the financial institution relevant to the reporting requirements of the Bank Secrecy Act. The financial institution could be required through a summons to produce at its own expense such documents and records at any location within 500 miles of the institution's place of business.

More Proposed Legislation

H.R. 3892, as introduced by Representative Wortly, would require the Secretary of the Treasury to review all exemption lists on an annual basis and, in a case of a change in bank control or management, the Secretary would be required to review the exemption list within 30 days. Additionally, H.R. 3892 would amend the Federal Deposit Insurance Act and the National Housing Act by extending the time frame within which supervisory agencies could review change of bank control applications for compliance with the Bank Secrecy Act.

Finally, H.R. 3892 would recycle the proceeds of seizures and forfeitures from any unlawful act back into the enforcement of the Bank Secrecy Act.

H.R. 4280, as introduced by Representative Torres, would increase the recordkeeping of financial institutions by requiring extensive records on all currency transactions of $3,000 or more to be kept for five years. This is an attempt to increase information available for investigations. This proposal will obviously increase the amount of records a financial institution will be required to keep; however, the utility of the proposal is unclear.

H.R. 4573, as introduced by Representative Pickle, would deal with the problem of structured transaction or "smurfing," by making it a crime to cause or attempt to cause a financial institution to fail to properly file a Currency Transaction Report on a transaction. Proceeds or property interests directly traceable to the failure to file would be subject to seizure or forfeiture. We believe H.R. 4573 is a cogent attempt to stem the evasive tactics of money launderers. It focuses everyone's attention on the motivation of the drug trafficker.

As mentioned above, "structuring" or "smurfing" allows criminals to exchange illegally derived monies for cashier's checks, traveler's checks, etc. Mr. Pickle's approach would subject persons to civil and criminal liability for causing or attempting to cause a domestic financial institution to "fail to file a (currency transaction) report", or to file the report with "a material omission or misstatement of fact" or structuring or assisting in structuring a transaction "for the purpose of evading the reporting requirements." This language will address the structured transaction problem which has forced the courts to dismiss charges against individuals who may have been involved in deliberate evasion of the Bank Secrecy Act reporting requirements.[1]

While there have been several cases that have found "structured transactions" in violation of 31 U.S.C. 5313(a)[2], the confusion over the statute and its implementing regulations needs to be solved once and for all; otherwise dismissals of charges such as that in the recent *United States v. Dela Espriella*[3] will continue.

Money Laundering Crimes and Disclosure Act

The ABA would like to suggest to this Committee another proposal, already offered in the Senate by Senator DeConcini, and very similar to Mr. Wortley's proposal in H.R. 3892, which would complement this Committee's response to tightening the Bank Secrecy Act. Senator DeConcini introduced S. 1385, the "Money Laundering Crimes and Disclosure Act" which deals in part with the reporting problem associated with currency transaction report exemptions. S. 1385 would amend 31 U.S.C. 5318, which gives the Secretary of the Treasury authority to "prescribe (or revoke) an appropriate exemption" by requiring the financial institution to provide to the Secretary of the Treasury (or his delegate) "a list of customers of the financial institution whose transactions have been exempted" and by further requiring the Secretary to "review and approve or revoke the list of exemptions within 90 days after the date of receipt." If the Secretary failed to notify the financial institution within the time provided, the exemption list would be deemed approved. These proposed changes would encourage frequent review of the CTR exemption lists and provide financial institutions with an incentive to internally review and update their lists. These reviews would guarantee that the lists are used only for their intended purposes: to exclude from the reporting requirements only those customers clearly intended to qualify under the regulations.

Additionally, we would like to suggest some new language relating to an internal audit of the financial institution. Specifically, a section such as the following should be added:

> No liability for a civil penalty shall be imposed upon a financial institution for a violation of this subchapter or a regulation prescribed under this subchapter if such violation is first discovered by such financial institution and is promptly disclosed by such financial institution to the Secretary or in accordance with regulations prescribed by the Secretary.

This amendment provides that liability for civil penalty will not be imposed upon the financial institution for violations of the Bank Secrecy Act or regulations thereunder if the financial institution discovers such violations and promptly discloses them to the Treasury Department. The purpose of this amendment is to encourage financial institutions to audit for Bank Secrecy Act compliance and to disclose and report negligent failure to comply with the Act. Without such a provision, the consequences to the institution would be the same whether violations were discovered in the course of an internal audit or an external examination. Since the amendment will induce financial institutions to ensure full compliance, it will further the general purposes of the Bank Secrecy Act.

Solutions Aimed at Curbing Drug Trafficking

There have been numerous proposed solutions aimed at curbing drug trafficking. The ABA supports the Chairman's goal of immediate, effective action. This goal can only be met by putting aside the all-encompassing proposals in the Administration's bill and by enacting the practical approach embodied in H.R. 4573. We believe that H.R. 4573 along with certain provisions in H.R. 1945 represent these universally acceptable solutions.

The penalties in H.R. 1945 attach to a domestic financial institution and a partner, director, officer, or employee of a domestic financial institution. H.R. 4573 extends the reach of penalties to persons outside the financial institution. Under H.R. 4573, any person who causes or attempts to cause a domestic financial institution to fail to file a report required by the Bank Secrecy Act or to file a report containing a material omission or misstatement of fact would be subject to civil penalties in the form of the forfeiture provisions. United States coin, currency, monetary instruments, or any other interest property traceable to such instruments, coin, or currency could be seized and forfeited to the U.S. government.

We believe the forfeiture proposal presents an issue that needs clarification: that is, the extent of the reach of forfeiture should be more precisely defined.

The forfeiture subsection covers funds and assets that are "traceable" to the coin or currency involved in a violation of the Bank Secrecy Act. The limits of the "reach" of forfeiture need to be clarified. Even though it is the intent of the proposal that no property or interest in property shall be forfeited if it can be established that the owner is a bona fide purchaser for value who took ownership without notice of the violation; or if the violation was not willful, the language offers no protection or immunity to innocent sellers or innocent parties to a transaction who accept collateral that may indeed be "traceable" to tainted funds. While the ABA supports the concept of forfeiture as a method of arresting the process of legitimization of illicit drug profits, we offer this support with a concern for the need to protect all innocent participants in legitimate business transactions.

Both H.R. 1945 and H.R. 4573, focus on subjecting violators of the Bank Secrecy Act to civil penalties, whether inside or outside of the financial institutions. H.R. 1945 would subject a bank and/or its personnel to civil penalties in the amount of the transaction for Bank Secrecy Act violations. Under H.R. 4573, a person who causes a particular violation of the Bank Secrecy Act can be penalized civilly in the amount of the transaction involved. Because both H.R. 1945 and H.R. 4573 amend Title 31 of the United States Code, the criminal penalties found in Section 5322 of Title 31 will not only apply to the bank and its personnel, but also to the person outside the bank. The amended Title 31, along with use of the new forfeiture provisions as set out in

H.R. 4573, gives the law enforcement community and financial institutions an effective weapon against two elements of the drug traffic—the person and the proceeds. . . .

As we have already stated, we do not believe there is any need to amend Title XI, the Right to Financial Privacy Act. Title VI, the Change in Bank Control provisions, has already been discussed in the context of H.R. 3892. We do not believe there is a need to make changes in Title I (Supervisory Powers) or in Title VI (Change of Bank Control) at this time. However, if the Congress and the Supervisory agencies believe changes are necessary to combat drug trafficking, we would be happy to work with Congress and the regulators on any possible changes.

---

[1] See *United States v. Anzalone,* 766 F.2d 676 (lst Cir. 1985), *United States v. Denemark,* 779 F.2d 1559 (11th Cir. 1986) and *United States v. Varbel,* 780 F.2d 758 (9th Cir. 1986) which have all held that structuring currency transactions to avoid the reporting requirements was not a crime. In fact, the court in the *Varbel* case pointed out that:

[I]f Congress or the Secretary wish to impose a reporting duty on financial institution customers, they must do so in clear, unambiguous language. We cannot impose the duty by implication.

[2] See *United States v. Tobon-Builes,* 709 F.2d 1092 (11th Cir. 1983) and *United States v. Thompson,* 603 F.2d 1200 (5th Cir. 1979).

[3] 781 F.2d 1432 (9th Cir. 1986). Here, an individual employed persons as "runners" who each day carried large sums of currency to various banks and converted the cash into cashier's checks or other negotiable instruments. The currency was apparently derived from cocaine trafficking. The court on the authority of the *Varbel* decision reversed the convictions on the charges of conspiracy to violate Section 5313.

The court concluded that "the currency reporting requirements of 31 U.S.C. 5313 do not apply to multiple transactions, each involving less than $10,000 but aggregating to make more than $10,000." 781 F.2d at 1438.

45

IMPROVING VOCABULARY

This activity may be used as an individualized study guide for students in libraries and resource centers or as a discussion catalyst in small group and classroom discussions.

The ability to understand an author's vocabulary is an essential reading skill. This skill is especially important when the vocabulary is specific to a particular social group, profession, or trade. Many of the authors in Chapter Two have used words that are understood by people who are involved with drug enforcement.

Guidelines

1. The words listed on the next page were used in the readings of Chapter Two. Define these words. (Most of the words are defined in the readings, but you may have to consult a dictionary to define others.)

2. See if you can locate sentences from the readings that use the words listed on the next page.

3. Create one sentence statements that use each of the words listed on the next page.

List of Words to Define

money laundering
narcodollar
transaction
drug trafficker
bearer bonds
dummy corporation
"over invoicing"
contraband
political insurgencies
precursor chemicals
slush funds
"smurfs"

CHAPTER 3

POLITICAL LEADERS
AND THE DRUG CARTEL

5 POLITICAL LEADERS AND THE DRUG CARTEL

THE REAGAN ADMINISTRATION'S COMPLICITY IN TRADING DRUGS

The Christic Institute

The Christic Institute is a non-profit, nonpartisan center for law and national policy in the public interest. The Institute's investigation has revealed that some of Oliver North's secret network of ex-CIA and military officers have been associated with large-scale drug trafficking in covert wars.

Points to Consider:

1. How did the guns-for-drugs operation work?
2. Offer three examples of contra involvement in drug smuggling.
3. Was the Reagan Administration aware of contra drug activity? Provide evidence to support your answer.
4. Who is John Hull? What role has he played in the contra-drug connection?

The Christic Institute, *A Christic Institute Special Report: The Contra-Drug Connection,* Washington, D.C., pp. 1-11.

The pilots who flew in the "guns-for-drugs" operation for the contras believe the Reagan Administration was fully aware and largely responsible for contra drug activity.

A major theme of the Reagan presidency in the 1980's has been the 'War on Drugs,' both at home and abroad. During her anti-drug crusade, Nancy Reagan has told America's youth to "Just Say No!" to drugs. Meanwhile, President Reagan and his law enforcement agencies have vowed to stem the flow of narcotics across the U.S. border and "control the problem at its source," namely, in the drug-exporting countries of Latin America.

Facing the Real Drug War

Astonishingly, however, over the past two years, mounting evidence has implicated the U.S.-backed Nicaraguan "contras"—President Reagan's so-called "freedom fighters" attempting to overthrow the government of Nicaragua—and their supporters in large-scale drug trafficking. Contra narcotics smuggling stretches from cocaine plantations in Colombia, to dirt airstrips in Costa Rica, to pseudo-seafood companies in Miami, and, finally, to the drug-ridden streets of our society.

The evidence suggests that not only were high Reagan Administration officials aware of contra drug trafficking, but some have attempted to cover up this fact and have directly assisted such illicit activity. Despite what has already been revealed by the Iran/contra scandal, the contra-drug connection and the potential U.S. government link to it remains one of the most underreported yet explosive stories of this decade.

The Evidence

Evidence of drug trafficking by the contras and their supporters centers on four related allegations: 1) that a major "guns-for-drugs" operation has existed between North, Central, and South America that has helped finance the contra war; 2) that the contra leadership has received direct funding and other support from major narcotics traffickers; 3) that some of the contra leaders have themselves been directly involved in drug trafficking; and 4) that United States government funds for the contras have gone to known narcotics dealers.

Guns-for-Drugs

Much attention has been focused on the secret resupply operation set up by the Reagan Administration to keep the contras armed when such assistance was outlawed by Congress between October 1984 and October 1986. Lesser known is that this resupply operation involved

DRUGS-FOR-GUNS: A U.S. GOVERNMENT ROLE?

Q: "Do you really believe the government decided to get into the drug business in order to pay for the contras? The American government?"

A: "As incredulous as it may sound, I believe that they not only decided to get into it, I think they orchestrated the whole thing."

> —Michael Tolliver,
> Contra drug pilot,
> to CBS News' "West 57th,"
> April 6, 1987

"They [the Reagan Administration] needed the financial support for the contras and it [drug sales] was one more way for them to obtain that financial support. The word came down from Washington, from the top, that no matter what has to be done in order to get money to supply the contras has got to be done."

> —George Morales,
> Drug smuggler who
> arranged contra drug
> smuggling operations,
> Quoted in *Out of Control*

"I smuggled my share of illegal substance, but I also smuggled my share of weapons [to the contras] in exchange, with the full knowledge and assistance of the DEA [Drug Enforcement Agency] and the CIA."

> —Gary Betzner,
> Contra drug pilot,
> *Newsweek*,
> January 26, 1987

The Christic Institute, *A Christic Institute Special Report: The Contra-Drug Connection*, Washington, D.C., pp. 1-11

not only sending arms down to the contras, but also bringing drugs—mostly cocaine—back into the United States. Profits from these drug sales were recycled to buy more weapons for the contras.

The guns-for-drugs operation worked as follows: Planeloads of Colombian cocaine were flown to farmlands in northern Costa Rica owned by an American rancher named John Hull. Hull has been iden-

51

Reprinted by permission of the *Star Tribune, Newspaper of the Twin Cities.*

tified as a CIA or National Security Council (NSC) liaison to the contras based in Costa Rica on the "Southern Front" of the U.S. war against Nicaragua. Several sources told Senator John Kerry's staff that Hull claimed in 1984 and 1985 to be receiving $10,000 a month from the NSC. (*"Private Assistance" and the Contras, A Staff Report,* Sen. John Kerry, October 14, 1986, p. 10. The Kerry Report mentioned 12 of the 29 Christic defendants originally named by the suit in May of 1986. Christic lawyers and investigators have shared their findings with Senator Kerry's staff.) The *Boston Globe* on July 20, 1986, quoted an intelligence source saying that Hull "was getting well paid and did what he was told to do" by the CIA. . . .

Other Reports of Contra Drug Trafficking

Over the past two years, a range of U.S. government and press reports have documented contra involvement in drug smuggling. These include:

• In May of 1985, the chief of the U.S. Drug Enforcement Agency in San Jose, Costa Rica, told local journalists: "We have reports that certain groups, under the pretext of running guns to the contra rebels, are smuggling drugs to the United States." (*Tico Times,* May 31, 1985)

52

- In March 1986, the *San Francisco Examiner* reported that a major cocaine ring broken up in 1983 had helped fund a Costa Rican-based contra organization. The "frogman" case was considered the biggest drug bust in West Coast history—430 pounds of cocaine was seized while being off-loaded from a Colombian freighter in San Francisco. The case's contra connection was covered up when court documents were sealed.

The *Examiner* story revealed that the U.S. government returned $36,020 that was seized as drug money to Julio Zavala, one of the convicted smugglers, because he submitted letters from contra leaders claiming it was political money "for the reinstatement of democracy in Nicaragua." Zavala testified that he delivered about $500,000 to one contra group, the Nicaraguan Democratic Union-Nicaraguan Revolutionary Armed Forces (UDN-FARN). The head of UDN-FARN, Fernando "El Negro" Chamorro, has been linked to drug trafficking and has worked closely with John Hull. (Kerry Report, p. 10)

- The most important person in the frogman case was a Nicaraguan expatriate named Norwin Meneses-Cantero, the brother of Somoza's chief of police for Managua. A Drug Enforcement Agency confidential report of February 6, 1984, described Meneses-Cantero as "the apparent head of a criminal organization responsible for smuggling kilogram quantities of cocaine into the United States." He is reputed to have bought a condominium for FDN military chief Enrique Bermudez in Miami. Meneses-Cantero also appeared at a contra fundraiser in San Francisco with contra leader Adolfo Calero in 1984. (*SF Examiner,* June 23, 1986)

- Testimony in the "frogman" case also implicated Horacio Pereira, a Nicaraguan contra supporter in Costa Rica. When Pereira was himself tried and convicted for drug trafficking in Costa Rica in 1986, the government produced wire-tapped phone conversations between Pereira and contra leader Juan Sebastian "Guachan" Gonzalez Mendiola, leader of a contra faction linked to John Hull's ranch. According to CBS News: "In the conversations the men discuss large amounts of cocaine they were sending to the United States. The wire-tapped phone calls show the drug dealers have ties to the highest level of leadership in Costa Rica." (CBS News, June 12, 1986)

- In May of 1986, ABC television correspondent Karen Burns reported that congressional investigators believed that "contras [had] smuggled shipments of cocaine in commercial shrimp boats from [Central America] to the Miami area."

- On January 20 of this year, the *New York Times* reported that "officials from several [U.S. government] agencies said that by early last fall [1986], the Drug Enforcement Administration office in Guatemala had compiled convincing evidence that the contra military supply operation was smuggling cocaine and marijuana."

• Last February, Jack Blum, a Special Counsel to the Senate Foreign Relations Committee investigating contra drug trafficking allegations, told the *Los Angeles Times:* "I believe that there is no question, based on the things that we have heard, that contras and the contra infrastructure have been involved in the cocaine trade and in bringing cocaine into Florida."

• The House Select Committee on Narcotics Abuse and Control, chaired by Rep. Charles Rangel (D-NY), submitted to U.S. Customs the names of 38 individuals and companies associated with the contras that may have been connected to drug smuggling. In a June 23 press release, Rangel said he received a letter from William Rosenblatt, acting Customs commissioner. "Customs reports," said Rangel, "that for 24 of the 38 individuals and companies we asked them to check, there is 'positive' information on the Customs computer indicating previous interest . . . in these people or companies. This initial check provides information that warrants further investigation about possible tie-ins between the contras, the individuals carrying out the contra supply mission and drug smuggling activities." . . .

A U.S. Government Connection?

After establishing the many links between the contra movement and drug trafficking, the more disturbing question remains: What did the Reagan Administration and U.S. government agencies know of contra drug activity? Did they "wink and nod" at such activity in order to keep the contras funded and armed during the Boland Amendment ban on U.S. aid to the contras? Did U.S. officials impede or obstruct investigations and prosecutions of these operations? Did any U.S. officials directly or indirectly—using private "cutouts"—assist or facilitate contra drug trafficking?

The first question is the easiest to answer. Documents released by the Iran/Contra Select Committee reveal that the Reagan Administration was and is well aware of drug trafficking activities by the contras:

• A CIA back-channel message to Oliver North from U.S. Ambassador to Costa Rica Lewis Tambs, dated March 28, 1986, has noted on it that contra drug leader Adolfo "'Popo' Chamorro is alleged to be involved in drug trafficking."

• An April 1, 1985, memo from Rob Owen to Oliver North describes one Costa Rican rebel leader, Jose Robelo (Chepon), with the words "potential involvement in drug running." Another contra leader, Sebastian Gonzalez (Wachan), was "now involved in drug running out of Panama," according to Owen.

54

- A February 10, 1986, memo to North from Owen identifies a DC-4 plane being used by the contras as "used at one time to run drugs, and part of the crew had criminal records. Nice group the Boys [the CIA] choose."

- Oliver North, during an August 9, 1985, meeting with Owen, wrote in his notes: "DC-6 which is being used for runs [to supply the contras] out of New Orleans is probably being used for drug runs into U.S."

These documents make clear Oliver North's knowledge of drug trafficking by contra leaders. One of them, Fernando "El Negro" Chamorro—who received about $500,000 from one of the men convicted in the "frogman" cocaine bust—was in fact promoted by Washington. Following the departure of contra leader Eden Pastora, who headed the largest contra group in Costa Rica, Chamorro was chosen by North and Owen to lead a unified "Southern Front" for the contras based in Costa Rica. Owen visited him in Costa Rica and wrote to North about Chamorro's military needs.

There is a fine line between U.S. officials merely knowing of contra drug trafficking and being complicit in such activity. The first charge is damning enough. At a minimum, the Reagan Administration has tolerated association with drug smugglers as a price for backing the contras. At worst, individuals and agencies within the U.S. government can be charged with shielding from justice or actively assisting contra drug trafficking as one more component of the secret program to keep the contras armed and funded when Congress cut off aid.

The pilots who flew in the "guns-for-drugs" operation for the contras believe the Reagan Administration was fully aware and largely responsible for contra drug activity. Some of the major players in Oliver North's private network—all of whom are cited as former or current employees or operatives for the CIA or the NSC—are at the heart of the contra-drug operation.

The most important link between the Reagan Administration and contra drug smuggling is John Hull, whose ranch lands served as the center of the arms-for-drugs operation. Hull had several meetings with Oliver North, according to the Tower Commission, and his name shows up repeatedly in North's handwritten notes. Hull has long been called a CIA operative—a charge he denied vehemently until recently admitting to receiving CIA funding. (*Washington Times,* July 24, 1987). Oliver North's personal liaison to the contras—Rob Owen—worked closely with Hull, the contras, Cuban-Americans, and mercenaries operating on his ranch. (See Kerry Report)

Two of Oliver North's key operatives in the contra air resupply operation based in El Salvador—Felix Rodriguez and Rafael "Chi Chi" Quintero—are implicated in contra drug dealing. As mentioned earlier, Rodriguez served as a conduit for distributing $10 million of Colombian cocaine money funneled to the contras. And Quintero—a veteran CIA contract agent and Christic Institute defendant—had two meetings with contra drug pilot Michael Tolliver to discuss Tolliver's operations. (CBS News, "West 57th," April 6, 1987)

Individuals flying or shipping drugs into the U.S. would appear to need some help from government agencies. The *Boston Globe* reported in April that between 50 and 100 flights that "had been arranged by the CIA took off from or landed at U.S. airports during the past two years without undergoing inspection" by the Customs Service. That same month CBS News reported that the CIA directly intervened when Customs detained indicted drug trafficker Michael Palmer on a flight back from Central America. Customs officials were told to drop the issue of Palmer's extensive drug connections.

Whether or not Oliver North or other U.S. officials *directly* assisted the contra/drug operation, it is clear that the Reagan Administration obstructed investigations into, or, at the very least, has been remarkably dilatory in prosecuting contra gun and drug running activities. Attorney General Edwin Meese and the U.S. Attorney in Miami, Leon Kellner, intervened to head off an investigation of illicit contra activities out of Miami. The Justice Department cover-up was intended to keep secret derogatory information about the contras and their backers at a time when the Congress was preparing to vote on contra aid in the spring of 1986. (Murray Waas and Joe Conason, *The Village Voice,* March 31, 1987)

In fact, contra drug smuggling raises serious questions for the entire U.S. government law enforcement apparatus. Such questions were posed by the National Security Archive, a Washington-based research group, in a July 6, 1987, memo to the Select Committee on Narcotics Abuse and Control:

"Were the field officers in Central America, the Caribbean, and the U.S. from the various agencies (DEA, Customs, Bureau of Alcohol, Tobacco, and Firearms, FBI) with jurisdiction over drug violations aware of the contra-drug allegations? If not, why not? If they were aware, where are their reports to their superiors? How did law enforcement officers not know or report these allegations when Robert Owen clearly knew and reported them to Oliver North? What, if any, investigations were ever undertaken into these allegations? What were the results of these investigations, if any? Were law enforcement officers ever directed not to investigate? What contacts, if any, did law enforcement officers have with other federal agencies, including the intelligence community, regarding these contra-drug allegations? Was the intelligence community involved in investigating these allegations?". . .

An Issue of Common Concern

U.S. government association with drug traffickers is not only the price paid for backing the contras, but, more generally, for engaging in covert operations around the world for the past 40 years. Covert operations are the ideal conduit for the drug trade and other criminal activity. Even when cloaked by patriotic appeals for achieving "freedom" and "democracy" abroad, covert operations invariably undermine our democracy at home. They subvert our values, our need for an open, honest, and accountable foreign policy, and respect for the rule of law.

6
POLITICAL LEADERS
AND THE DRUG CARTEL

THE CARTER ADMINISTRATION'S
COMPLICITY IN TRADING DRUGS

M. Stanton Evans

M. Stanton Evans wrote the following reading in his capacity as a contributing editor for Human Events, *a national conservative weekly.*

Points to Consider:

1. For how many years has the Panamanian government been running drugs?
2. Who was Moises Torrijos and what role did he play in drug trafficking during the 1970's?
3. What happened to DEA reports and files on Panamanian drug trafficking?
4. Why did the Carter Administration conceal information about the Panamanian dictatorship's involvement in drug trafficking?

M. Stanton Evans, "How Panama Drug Traffic Was Covered Up," *Human Events,* April 2, 1988, p. 296. Reprinted with permission.

There was at the time considerable evidence that Panamanian officials were involved in drugs and other unseemly activities, but that facts about the subject were suppressed by the regime of Jimmy Carter.

The February indictment of Gen. Manuel Antonio Noriega—and the concerted U.S. attempt to topple him from power—have suddenly made it fashionable to talk in public about drug-running by the government of Panama.

Most news accounts about the asserted misdeeds of Gen. Noriega suggest that these are recently discovered problems, and that U.S. authorities moved directly to clear the matter up as soon as they were told about it. The Panamanian connection, the casual reader might suppose, has only recently come to our attention.

Nothing, as it happens, could be further from the truth. High-level involvement by the government of Panama in running drugs is very old news indeed—reported 10 years and more ago. It has been known to U.S. officials for even longer than that, and anybody in a relevant position of authority who didn't know about it must have been sleeping on the job.

A Systematic Cover-up

The American people, on the other hand, have plenty of reason to be astonished by the current revelations, since the Panamanian connection has been the subject of a systematic cover-up, engineered by people in our government and assisted by an indifferent press corps who (with a couple of honorable exceptions) couldn't be bothered to tell the story. The effects of this concealment, up to and possibly including the destruction of official records, are with us still.

At the center of this melodrama were Noriega's predecessor strongman, Gen. Omar Torrijos and his family, who were the people to whom we turned over the Panama Canal in 1978. There was at the time considerable evidence that the Torrijos family and other Panamanian officials (including Noriega, then a Torrijos subaltern) were involved in drugs and other unseemly activities, but the facts about the subject were suppressed by the regime of Jimmy Carter.

The Panama Connection

Data about the Panama connection had been accumulating in the files of senators, congressmen, and the executive branch at least since the early 1970's, indicating that heroin and cocaine that made their way into the United States in many cases were transiting through Panama, with the connivance of Panamanian officials. Various details of this connection—and related cover-up—were reported at the time of the Panama Canal debate.

One of the matters discussed in those reports was the fact that Torrijos' brother, Moises (who was also an official of the government), was under indictment in the early 1970's for involvement with heroin smuggling in New York, and that a bench warrant had been issued for his arrest. This embarrassing state of affairs may have had something to do with the fact that Moises—though head of treaty information—didn't show up in the United States for the treaty-signing ceremony that began conveying the Panama Canal to his brother's government.

That Moises and other Panamanians were subject to this indictment was certainly known to American officials—so much so, in fact, that a State Department functionary was able to tip him off in advance, thereby permitting him to evade arrest (this happened in December 1972, according to the Senate Intelligence Committee, suggesting that our problems in this respect predate not only the current Noriega flap but also the Jimmy Carter era). Moreover, this was only one of several cases in which Panamanian officials were indicted for running drugs.

Carter Administration Concealed Information

Beyond all this, there were numerous reports in the files of the Drug Enforcement Administration (DEA) concerning allegations that not only Moises but numerous other Panamanian higher-ups, including Omar himself, were involved in trafficking with drugs. Assertions about these and other such files were made by Sen. Robert Dole, Sen. Jesse Helms, then-Rep. John Murphy, and others. When the Carter Administration stonewalled on making the records available, Sen. Dole and Phil Jones of CBS News (one of the few reporters in the major media to dig in on this story) filed a Freedom of Information request to get the relevant data.

"YEAH, I USED TO BE A LATIN AMERICAN DICTATOR, BUT I FOUND THE PAY, THE HOURS, THE FRINGE BENEFITS AND THE JOB SECURITY WERE MUCH BETTER IN DRUGS!..."

Cartoon by Doug Marlette. By permission of Doug Marlette, Atlanta Constitution.

When some files were at last turned over, they had been so thoroughly gutted that nothing much could be discovered from them. All that could be told for certain was that somebody had gone through the pages and systematically blacked out any and all references to the Torrijos family (for instance, the Moises Torrijos case discussed above was mentioned in the files, along with the names of other people indicted, but Moises' name had been blacked out.)

The motives of the Carter Administration in concealing information about the Panamanian dictatorship were not, of course, mysterious. Well-publicized charges about the involvement of the Torrijos family and other Panamanian officials in such traffic could well have torpedoed any chance for ratifying the canal treaties, which was a paramount goal of the Carter government in 1977-78.

Under Ronald Reagan, however, no such motives should exist, and it occurred to me that it might now be possible to get uncensored copies of the DEA files in question, to find out what was denied to us back then. Accordingly, I asked researcher Ashley Landess of the National Journalism Center to see if the current DEA would now provide the files. The answer she got back was that the files—for reasons that are a bit unclear—have unfortunately been destroyed.

In fact, Landess encountered a consistent pattern of missing documents and official amnesia on this topic. The Senate Intelligence Committee report referred to above, we were told, did not exist (it does;

we have it). The House Merchant Marine Committee had no knowledge of a report that it compiled about the subject in 1973 (we also have this).

Why Senate and House committees know so little of their own reports about this subject is something of a puzzle. In the case of the executive branch, it is pretty clear that we are dealing with deliberate concealment at the time of the Carter presidency—in order to facilitate the passage of the Panama Canal treaties. While we are worrying about the integrity of the Panamanian government, it looks as if we would also be advised to worry about the integrity of our own.

7 POLITICAL LEADERS AND THE DRUG CARTEL

SAYING YES TO DRUGS: CRIMES TAINT U.S. LEADERS PAST AND PRESENT

Peter G. Bourne

Peter G. Bourne wrote the following reading in his capacity as special assistant to the president in the Carter White House. He was also responsible for international drug-control policy.

Points to Consider:

1. Why are important segments of the foreign policy bureaucracy reluctant to expose the drug involvement of top leaders of other countries?
2. In what other countries, besides Panama, have U.S. officials tolerated large-scale drug trafficking by political leaders?
3. Summarize the reasons why U.S. officials are "saying yes" to foreign leaders' drug trafficking. Of what value are these leaders to U.S. interests?
4. Why, then, did the United States move against Panama's Manuel Noriega?

Peter G. Bourne, "Hypocrisy in the Battle Against Drugs," *Star Tribune,* March 29, 1988, p. 11A. Copyright © 1988 by The New York Times Company. Reprinted by permission.

If Washington truly wants to stop international drug trafficking, we cannot apply the law selectively.

Federal government officials have been aware of Gen. Manuel Noriega's involvement in drug trafficking for more than 10 years. Their failure to act reflects a persistent schizophrenia in the government that has long hampered efforts to stem the flow of drugs from Latin America into this country.

In 1977, a sealed indictment for involvement in drug trafficking was handed down against the brother of Gen. Omar Torrijos, the former Panamanian strongman and Noriega's boss at the time. Justice Department officials planned to arrest him when his plane landed in the Canal Zone on his return from an overseas trip. During a stopover in Venezuela, he was warned of the trap by a State Department official and, by changing his itinerary, avoided arrest.

Tolerating Large-scale Drug Trafficking

Such stories are legion. Despite Reagan administration assertions of a fervent desire to "say no to drugs" by putting an end to the international drug traffic, the clear message has been that our government is divided, with important segments of the foreign policy bureaucracy reluctant to expose the drug involvement of top officials of other countries in order to protect professed national-security interests.

Some foreign policy professionals in the administration have long considered that the cooperation of tainted leaders in the hemisphere on a host of political issues ultimately transcends our concern about drugs exported to this country.

As a result, despite overwhelming evidence we have been willing for years to tolerate large-scale drug trafficking by the families of heads of state, top government officials and insurgent groups we have supported. In addition to Panama, this has been true in Antigua, the Bahamas, Colombia, El Salvador, Haiti, Honduras, Jamaica, Mexico, and Paraguay.

Most recently, boldly confronting the contras' drug trafficking was deemed too damaging to the lofty goal of presenting them as "comparable to our Founding Fathers." And there is also strong evidence that some U.S. officials knowingly closed their eyes to the contras' shipping of drugs into this country as a way of helping generate funds.

Turning a Blind Eye to Drugs

In the world of realpolitik, the diplomatic and intelligence communities still look askance at the idea that the drug issue ranks on a par with the major geopolitical struggles around which their careers revolve. They view drugs first and foremost as a domestic public-relations problem.

64

THE WAR ON DRUGS

Theodore Roosevelt, the greatest Republican president of the century, said he believed in speaking softly and carrying a big stick. When it comes to the war on drugs, this administration [the Reagan Administration] speaks loudly and carries a twig.

Haynes Johnson, Star Tribune, *June 1, 1988*

Turning a blind eye to the immense profits being made by foreign leaders and their friends and relatives is still seen as a small price to pay—provided these individuals remain fully responsive to the Reagan administration's regional ideological goals.

Indeed, many in their intelligence community have viewed this form of benign neglect as an easy way to buy collaboration without having to spend a single dollar of taxpayers' money.

Key officials also feel it gives them an important degree of leverage when foreign nationals are compromised by our awareness of their criminal activities. A thoroughly honest and uncorruptible individual is of modest value to a U.S. operative.

Often those most corrupted are, like Noriega, powerful figures in their countries' intelligence or military establishments. Their value to our interests is seen as far exceeding any benefit to be gained by removing them because of their involvement in the narcotics trade.

Applying the Law Selectively

The belated move against Noriega came not because of any sudden discovery of his longstanding involvement with drugs but because of the perception of his diminished utility in the pursuit of the administration's Central American policy.

If Washington truly wants to stop international drug trafficking, we cannot apply the law selectively, exempting some foreign leaders merely because they are seen to be responsive to another, often covert agenda.

This means interagency strife must end. Some agencies must not be allowed to protect old "friends" and thus undermine others that are committed to ending the drug scourge.

65

Cartoon by David Seavey. Copyright 1988, *USA Today*. Reprinted with permission.

POLITICAL LEADERS
AND THE DRUG CARTEL

SAYING NO TO DRUGS:
FIGHTING
THE INTERNATIONAL CARTEL

David D. Queen

*David D. Queen presented the following testimony before the House
of Representatives Select Committee on Narcotics Abuse and Control in his capacity as Deputy Assistant Secretary (Enforcement) at
the Department of Treasury.*

Points to Consider:

1. Describe the methods that the Treasury Department uses to detect
   illegal drug trafficking and money laundering.
2. How much money was shipped from Panama to the U.S. between
   1980-1984?
3. Why is Panama particularly vulnerable to money launderers?

Excerpted from testimony of David D. Queen before the House of
Representatives Select Committee on Narcotics Abuse and Control,
June 19, 1986.

President Reagan has identified the interdiction of illegal drugs as one of the major priorities of this administration.

The Treasury Department is pleased to have this opportunity to address the issue of international drug trafficking, narcotics-related money laundering, and other activities associated with the illicit narcotics trade.

Top Priority: Drug Enforcement

In the past decade illegal drug trafficking has increased dramatically, with a corresponding increase in crimes associated with it. President Reagan has identified the interdiction of illegal drugs as one of the major priorities of this administration. In support of this commitment the United States has allocated substantial law enforcement and prosecutorial resources to impede the flow of drugs and moneys associated with this illegal activity across our borders. As you may be aware, the Treasury Department and its law enforcement agencies has taken an equally firm stand to put narcotics interdiction squarely at the top of our international law enforcement agenda. We have repeatedly stated in every available forum that drug trafficking is a problem that cannot be solved by any one person, agency, or government. It must be attacked on all fronts and with every tool at our command, including the cooperation and assistance of our allies.

The Treasury Department has primary responsibility for enforcing the "Bank Records and Foreign Transactions Act," commonly referred to as the "Bank Secrecy Act." The Act authorizes the Secretary of the Treasury to require certain reports and records where they are unlikely to have a high degree of usefulness in criminal, tax, or regulatory investigations or proceedings. Under the Act, Treasury is responsible for monitoring the flow of currency in and out of the United States through the use of the reporting requirements. In addition, this law permits us to monitor and require the reporting of large cash transactions at domestic financial institutions.

Trying to Detect Money Laundering

Our experience in this area indicates that illegal drug trafficking, and the money laundering associated with it, require the use of sophisticated financial arrangements involving the movement of large sums of cash. In many instances the financial institutions and systems that are used for these activities have no knowledge that they are being used to launder money.

Early in 1983, the Treasury Department became aware of an unusual flow of U.S. currency from the Banco Nacional de Panama (National Bank of Panama) to the Federal Reserve Bank offices in New York and

Miami. Based on the data we were able to compile, it revealed that from 1980 through 1984 approximately $3.5 billion (primarily small bills) was shipped from Panama to the United States. In contrast the Federal Reserve Banks shipped to Panama $500 million in replacement currency during the same period, showing an immense cash surplus. Although U.S. government agencies had received information for a number of years indicating that major drug traffickers or money launderers were using Panamanian banks or shell corporations to conceal their financial transactions, we were previously unaware of the magnitude and growth of the transactions being channeled through Panama.

Although our most recent data indicates the currency flow from the Banco Nacional de Panama appears to have decreased, it is still running at a very high level. It is our belief, based on data from the Forms 4789 (Currency Transaction Report—IRS) and 4790 (Currency & Monetary Instruments Report—Customs) filed with us, that much of this money is from illegal activities, mainly drug trafficking.

Panama: A Vulnerable Spot

Panama is particularly vulnerable to money launderers for two reasons: geography and its banking system. Geographically Panama is the crossroad between the two continents, North and South America. With the exception of Mexican marijuana and heroin, which are produced adjacent to its market, Central America and the many islands in the Caribbean provide the bridge traveled by Latin American drugs en route to markets in the United States and Europe.

Cartoon by Richard Wright. Reprinted with permission.

In the opposite direction a stream of money flows back to reimburse participants at the various stages of the production and trafficking process and to pay for the equipment and protection needed to move the various products to their destinations.

The flow pattern of drug money is motivated by many of the same considerations that govern the disposition of other liquid assets. Like legitimate money, narcodollars tend to seek the highest rate of return and the lowest rate of taxation consistent with other considerations, such as secrecy and the ease with which narcodollars may be disguised as legitimate dollars. While Panama is smaller geographically and in population than the State of New Jersey, it has over 123 banks operating within its borders, and can justifiably proclaim itself the major financial center for Latin America. Approximately 70 of these financial institutions are associated with 26 foreign countries, including: U.S.—14, Japan—9, France—6, Switzerland—5, Canada—3, Colombia—2, etc. The facilities through which narcodollars may be laundered or disguised as legitimate dollars are abundant.

A common hazard shared by drug traffickers is fluctuation in the relative value of currencies. Since the most likely exchange rate movement is devaluation of nonconvertible currency, traffickers try to hold their funds in hard currency (preferably U.S. dollars) as long as possible. The balboa, the Panamanian unit of currency, is at par with and equivalent to the U.S. dollar. Panama issues no paper currency. The U.S. dollar serves as the circulating medium of paper currency, making it almost impossible to segregate narcodollars from legitimate dollars.

Drug money movements are susceptible to special problems. Like illicit drugs, narcodollars are a form of contraband, which places an exceptionally high premium on secrecy of movement. It is no secret that Panama has perhaps the most stringent bank secrecy laws of any country in the region. Indeed, much of its success as a banking center is directly attributable to the strict confidentiality inherent in its bank secrecy laws and numbered accounts which are major ingredients in the system.

Progress Is Being Made

While the picture I have painted may appear somewhat dismal, I am pleased to report that we are engaged in discussions aimed at addressing these problems. During my tenure as Deputy Assistant Secretary I have had the opportunity to discuss this problem with my law enforcement colleagues at the Justice and State Departments, and our counterparts within the government of Panama. The Panamanians have built a record of informal cooperation and assistance to the United States in law enforcement matters (e.g., extradition, search, and seizure of Panamanian flag-ships, etc.). It is clear that illegal drug trafficking has important implications for the national interest of our respective countries. I believe this concern is shared by civilian officials at the highest level of the Panamanian government with whom we have dealt. Building on the tradition of informal law enforcement cooperation that Panama has established, I am hopeful that as our discussions continue the United States and Panama will be able to develop a framework through which this problem may be addressed.

INTERPRETING
EDITORIAL CARTOONS

This activity may be used as an individualized study guide for students in libraries and resource centers or as a discussion catalyst in small group and classroom discussions.

Although cartoons are usually humorous, the main intent of most political cartoonists is not to entertain. Cartoons express serious social comment about important issues. Using graphics and visual arts, the cartoonist expresses opinions and attitudes. By employing an entertaining and often light-hearted visual format, cartoonists may have as much or more impact on national and world issues as editorial and syndicated columnists.

Points to Consider:

1. Examine the cartoon in this activity. (See next page.)

2. How would you describe the message of this cartoon? Try to describe the message in one to three sentences.

3. Do you agree with the message expressed in this cartoon? Why or why not?

4. Does the cartoon support the author's point of view in any of the readings in this book? If the answer is yes, be specific about which reading or readings and why.

5. Are any of the readings in Chapter Three in basic agreement with this cartoon?

CHAPTER 4

CONTROLLING
THE DRUG EPIDEMIC

Stopping Domestic Use

CONTROLLING
THE DRUG EPIDEMIC

CONTROLLING DRUG ABUSE:
AN OVERVIEW

General Accounting Office

The following statement was excerpted from a special report from the Comptroller General of the United States. The report, entitled Controlling Drug Abuse: A Status Report, *is intended to provide an overview of the drug problem and federal response and to help people better understand the nature and dimensions of the drug problem and federal anti-drug efforts.*

General Accounting Office, *Controlling Drug Abuse: A Status Report*, Gaithersburg, Maryland, pp. 1-2.

How to Control Drug Abuse

Opinions vary about what the federal government should do to control drug abuse. Experts disagree about which anti-drug programs work best, the proper mix of anti-drug programs, and the level of resources needed to make anti-drug efforts successful. Some experts believe that devoting more resources—money, personnel, and equipment—to law enforcement will reduce the supply of drugs available for use. Others say we must increase our efforts to eradicate drug production in foreign countries and shut off supplies at their source. An increasing number of experts believe that a higher priority and more resources must be assigned to reducing the demand for drugs through programs aimed at preventing drug abuse, treating drug abusers, and conducting research on the causes and cures of drug abuse. Some experts believe that substantial reductions in drug abuse will not occur unless there are fundamental changes in cultural attitudes and values which decrease society's demand for illegal drugs.

Obstacles to Drug Abuse Control

During the 1980's, the General Accounting Office has issued to Congress over 40 reports and has presented numerous testimonies on various aspects of the government's efforts to combat the drug problem. The results of our work do not provide clear-cut answers as to the appropriate mix of anti-drug programs or the priority and level of resources which the federal government should devote to drug abuse control. Such decisions are exceedingly difficult to make and require a broad focus and synthesis of the government's efforts. Unfortunately, the ability of Congress and the executive branch to effectively address the overall issue is greatly hampered by the absence of factual information about which anti-drug programs work best. Existing data systems portray general drug trends and help gauge the overall impact of the federal drug strategy but do not adequately measure the effectiveness of specific federal drug control efforts. Moreover, despite numerous organizational changes, fragmented and uncoordinated anti-drug policies and programs remain obstacles to the success of federal drug abuse control efforts.

We have repeatedly pointed out problems caused by the fragmentation of federal anti-drug efforts among several cabinet departments and agencies and the resulting lack of coordination of federal drug abuse control policies and programs. Differing agency priorities, interagency rivalries, conflicts, and jurisdictional disputes have impeded drug abuse control efforts in the past, and continue to present obstacles to the success of the government's anti-drug programs. Congress and the executive branch have made several organizational changes over the past 20 years aimed at reducing fragmentation. But those changes have not succeeded in resolving conflicts among federal anti-drug policies and programs.

INTERNATIONAL STRATEGY

The U.S. government international strategy sets forth policy goals which, when carried out by U.S. government agencies and foreign governments, can lead to a reduction in drug production, trafficking, and abuse. The goals are to:

—Reduce the amount of cocaine, heroin, and marijuana entering the U.S. from foreign sources;
—Decrease tolerance for illicit drugs and stimulate support for effective worldwide narcotics control through public diplomacy initiatives;
—Eliminate major drug trafficking networks and cartels through increased seizure and arrests, prosecutions, and forfeiture of assets; and
—Secure increased international cooperation in worldwide narcotics control matters through diplomatic and program initiatives.

"International Narcotics Control," gist *(Bureau of Public Affairs/Department of State), June 1988*

Coordinating a Federal Anti-drug Policy

Additional organizational changes, such as the proposed establishment of a Director of National Drug Control Policy, may help. Organizational changes by themselves, however, are insufficient to accomplish the goal of stronger leadership and more centralized oversight and coordination of federal anti-drug policy. Such changes can succeed only if they are accompanied by a firm and continuing commitment by the President and Congress to resolve conflicts in the government's anti-drug programs.

Cartoon by David Seavey. Copyright 1985, *USA Today.* Reprinted with permission.

CONTROLLING
THE DRUG EPIDEMIC

MAKING PROGRESS
IN THE WAR ON DRUGS

Stephen S. Trott

Stephen S. Trott presented the following testimony in his capacity as Associate Attorney General of the United States Department of Justice. Mr. Trott is also chairman of the National Drug Policy Board's Law Enforcement Coordinating Group.

Points to Consider:

1. Describe the role of United States Attorneys in the Federal Drug Law Enforcement program.
2. Who are the OCDETF's? How will new resources from the Anti-Drug Abuse Act assist the OCDETF program?
3. Summarize the duties of the United States Marshals Service. What percentage of the marshals' workload is drug-related?
4. Why will the Anti-Drug Abuse Act have an effect on the federal prison system?

Excerpted from testimony of Stephen S. Trott before the House of Representatives Select Committee on Narcotics Abuse and Control, March 18, 1987.

By all measures, the program has been an outstanding success.

I will discuss the Justice Department's implementation of the Anti-Drug Abuse Act of 1986 and, more specifically, the impact this legislation has had—and will continue to have—on the 93 United States Attorneys' offices, the Organized Crime Drug Enforcement Task Force program, the U.S. Marshals Service, and the Federal Bureau of Prisons.

The Anti-Drug Abuse Act (ADAA) and related appropriations legislation provided the federal drug law enforcement and education/prevention communities with massive new legal, material, and manpower resources. With these new resources have come parallel increases in responsibility.

This expansion in resources and responsibilities has been welcomed by officials at the Justice Department, and particularly by those agencies which provide the investigators, prosecutors, and prison custodians actively engaged in making the nation's drug program work. It is to the roles, responsibilities, resources, and future of these vital members of the drug law enforcement community that I will now turn my attention.

United States Attorneys: Prosecuting Drug-related Cases

The 93 United States Attorneys serve as principal Justice Department representatives in federal judicial districts throughout the country. Their primary role in the Federal Drug Law Enforcement program is to prosecute drug-related cases in federal court and participate in coordinating major drug investigations. U.S. Attorneys, in short, represent the Justice Department's prosecutorial front line in the national battle against drug production, trafficking, and abuse.

U.S. Attorneys currently have over 6,500 drug-related matters underway involving almost 11,000 suspect-defendants. In addition, U.S. Attorneys have over 6,300 cases pending which have produced indictments or charges by complaint involving over 12,500 defendants. Although Anti-Drug Abuse Act implementation remains in its early stages, it is expected that the new legal resources provided in the Act will significantly increase their caseloads. . . .

As a result of the effective implementation of new legal and manpower resources, U.S. Attorneys expect significant progress. It is anticipated that the Act's mandatory minimum sentence provisions will generate an increase in the number of prosecutions going to trial, as defense attorneys may be less inclined to plead their clients guilty. Conversely, these provisions may provide a greater incentive for subjects to cooperate with government officials.

Furthermore, the Act's asset forfeiture provisions have expanded the government's authority in this area. Assets derived from illicit drug trafficking will be more susceptible to forfeiture as a result. Under the direction of the policy board coordinating group, interagency agreements are being prepared to ensure effective use of forfeited funds. Congress will be advised of the precise nature of finalized agreements, as one of the 58 reporting requirements of the Act. Seizing drug-related assets has unquestionably enhanced the government's ability to destroy the financial structure of drug trafficking groups.

OCDETF's: Fighting Organized Crime

In partnership with U.S. Attorneys are the Organized Crime Drug Enforcement Task Forces, or OCDETF's. Through a network of 13 regional offices in major U.S. cities, the goal of the OCDETF program is to identify, investigate, and prosecute members of high-level drug trafficking organizations, destroying their operations in the process. . . .

The OCDETF program has been highly successful in the four years since its start, producing over 3,300 indictments for drug-related offenses and over 5,300 convictions as a result of task force investigations. More convictions have been realized under the Career Criminal Enterprise Statute through this program than in all other efforts by the federal government in the last four years. By all measures, then, the OCDETF program has been an outstanding success.

As is the case with U.S. Attorneys, the most significant new resources the Anti-Drug Abuse Act offers the OCDETF program are new laws; federal agents and prosecutors are actively using these enhanced provisions in support of the OCDETF mission. . . .

It is expected that the OCDETF program's continued and effective implementation of these new resources will result in:

- More substantial sentences for convicted major traffickers;

- Substantial improvements in targeting the financial resources of drug traffickers and their associates;

- Increased cooperation from drug trafficking organization members at all levels due to the risk of longer periods of imprisonment;

- An improved ability to stem the outward flow of ill-gotten profits; and

- Greater success in extradition and extraterritorial drug and money laundering investigations.

Greater investigative and prosecutorial success on the part of U.S. Attorneys and the Organized Crime Drug Enforcement Task Forces will, in turn, mean a more active role for the United States Marshals Service in the Federal Drug Law Enforcement program.

Marshals Service: Ensuring Safety of the Judicial Process

Maintaining the safety and integrity of the judicial process is the Marshals Service's highest priority. In support of that objective, the Marshals must ensure the safety of the judiciary and endangered witnesses, execute warrants and court orders, manage seized assets, and handle prisoners awaiting sentencing. . . .

Currently almost 40 percent of the marshals' workload is drug-related. Effective implementation of the legal and manpower resources provided by the Anti-Drug Abuse Act will, necessarily, increase this figure.

For example, accelerated efforts to bring high-level drug traffickers to trial will result in a need for greater security precautions. The marshals spent $300,000 to insure the integrity of the recent "Pizza Connection" heroin case* proceedings, and it is expected that the upcoming Carlos Lehder-Rivas trial will require the most intense security ever afforded for the prosecution of a single criminal.

In addition, more high-level drug trafficking cases will require an appropriate expansion of the marshals' highly successful witness protection program. The recent murder of Barry Seal, a major drug witness who refused the program, demonstrates the lengths trafficking organization will go to block significant testimony.

Drug traffickers, the most violence-prone of all classes of criminals, pose a particular danger to investigative agents who develop incriminating evidence on which arrest warrants are based. Those agents and U.S. marshals, who may be called upon to execute warrants, regularly face life-threatening situations from drug violators intent on avoiding apprehension. Last year, approximately 20 percent of all arrests made by the Marshals Service were for drug-related offenses.

Finally, more investigations and prosecutions will increase the demands placed on the Marshals Service for the efficient control of prisoners. Currently, 90,000 prisoners are received annually, and on an average each prisoner has three to four court appearances. As major drug and organized crime figures are apprehended, greater reliance

---

*Editor's note: The "Pizza Connection" was the result of a five-year FBI investigation that focused on heroin importation and distribution and money laundering by Sicilian Mafia figures in association with the La Cosa Nostra in the U.S. The media commonly referred to the case as the "Pizza Connection" because the Mafia used pizza parlors throughout New York and five other states to facilitate the distribution of an estimated $1.65 billion worth of heroin smuggled into the U.S. from Sicily.

will be placed on the national prisoner transportation system. In addition, added pressures will be placed on the marshals to find short-term facilities to house prisoners.

Moving along the law enforcement continuum, if U.S. Attorneys, the Organized Crime Drug Enforcement Task Forces, and the Marshals Service all implement their respective Anti-Drug Abuse Act resources effectively, the Federal Bureau of Prisons will, in turn, have an expanded role in the drug law enforcement program.

Federal Bureau of Prisons: Carrying Out the Judgments

The Federal Bureau of Prisons is responsible for carrying out the judgments of federal courts whenever a period of confinement is ordered. The population of the Bureau's 47 institutions is now 42,000—50 percent above the total rated capacity of the federal prison system.

At present, drug law violators account for the largest segment of the inmate population—37 percent. This is in sharp contrast to 1970, when this figure was just 16 percent. The number of drug violators is expected to increase substantially with implementation of the Anti-Drug Abuse Act.

To house these new prisoners the Congress provided funding for two federal prisons. A site for a 700-bed federal correctional institution in Jesup, Georgia, has been located for one of these facilities. Construction of this $45 million facility will begin this summer and is scheduled to be completed in September 1989. Sites in the northeast and southeast are now being considered for another medium-security federal correctional institution.

Despite these new resources, the effect of the Anti-Drug Abuse Act on the federal prison system will be considerable. Currently, drug offenders serve 40 percent of the sentences imposed by the courts. Under the Act, drug offenders will serve mandatory minimum sentences, ranging from five to 20 years depending on the severity of the offense. These longer sentences will increase the length of time an offender will spend in federal prison, further increasing the population of the federal prison system.

The initial impact of the Act will be felt in 1990, when drug offenders imprisoned for crimes classified in the medium severity range would normally be released. Instead of serving approximately two years of a five-year sentence, these offenders will serve the full five years. Inmates in the high severity drug offense category now serve an average of four years of a ten-year sentence.

The severe shortage in prison space is a serious weakness in the overall criminal justice system. Despite the infusion of additional funds, as provided by the Anti-Drug Abuse Act, inmate overcrowding under current conditions appears inevitable. It is projected that by 1993 the total federal prison system population will be approximately 93 percent greater than the system's rated capacity. The President's 1988 budget proposes significant new funding to alleviate this problem. In addition, the policy board commissioned a working group, chaired by a representative of the Department of Justice, to explore a wide variety of possible solutions.

The benefits offered by the Anti-Drug Abuse Act, as I have indicated, carry with them considerable associated burdens for the law enforcement community. The nation must not compromise with drug trafficking and abuse, and we are prepared to shoulder these burdens.

CONTROLLING
THE DRUG EPIDEMIC

LOSING THE WAR ON DRUGS

Charles B. Rangel

Charles B. Rangel submitted the following prepared statement in his capacity as chairman of the House of Representatives Select Committee on Narcotics Abuse and Control. Mr. Rangel presided over hearings on drug law enforcement and interdiction under the Anti-Drug Abuse Act of 1986.

Points to Consider:

1. Why does the author disagree with the President's proposed budget?
2. What is the National Drug Policy Board?
3. Describe the variety of resources and equipment provided by the Anti-Drug Abuse Act of 1986. How will these resources enhance our drug-related intelligence capacity?
4. Summarize the reductions President Reagan made in federal drug enforcement and interdiction. What kind of effect will these cuts have on the war against drugs?

Excerpted from a prepared statement of Charles B. Rangel before the House of Representatives Select Committee on Narcotics Abuse and Control, March 18, 1987.

Our failure to act in the past has resulted in a flood of drugs into this country from abroad. . . . Our enforcement and interdiction efforts must be more than a matter of luck or accident.

The Anti-Drug Abuse Act of 1986 was a milestone in the war against drug trafficking and abuse. Underlying this legislation is a comprehensive national drug policy that addresses all aspects of the problem.

The members of the House Select Committee on Narcotics Abuse and Control worked hard to develop and secure passage of the Anti-Drug Abuse Act of 1986. We sought to provide the resources essential to waging a successful war against drugs. We remember the events of October 27, 1986, the day the bill was signed. We remember the commitment we made to the American people.

We Need a Long-term Commitment of Resources

I am afraid, however, that the President does not recall the promises of October 27. His proposed 1988 budget suggests that he does not recall his promises. Drug abuse education, treatment, state and local drug enforcement funds, as well as money for federal drug law enforcement and interdiction efforts have all been reduced for fiscal year 1988.

An effective response to our nation's drug problem will require a long-term commitment of resources. It cannot be won in a year, or even two.

The costs of this policy are so clear. Estimates are that the social and economic costs of drug abuse prevention, treatment, related crime, violence, death, and property destruction, lost productivity, and drug enforcement will total an additional $100 billion.

Our failure to act in the past has resulted in a flood of drugs into this country from abroad, and the deluge continues. The Select Committee estimates that in 1986, 178 tons of cocaine were directed at the United States. This compares to 143 tons in 1985 and 115.7 tons in 1984. An estimated 12 tons of heroin entered the U.S. in 1986.

Although the Coast Guard reports a significant increase in seizures of marijuana coming from Colombia, the Select Committee estimates that between 30,000 and 60,000 tons of marijuana are still being smuggled into the United States annually. During 1986, the estimated level of hashish smuggled into the United States remained at 200 tons.

In 1987, we can expect the flow of drugs directed at the United States to continue to increase. The State Department has reported bumper crops for 1986. Cocaine, marijuana, hashish, and heroin will inundate our borders from the air, sea, and land.

Until the day that we can stem the tide of drugs at the source through diplomacy and effective and aggressive eradication programs, a major commitment to interdiction and federal drug law enforcement is critical

to an effective comprehensive anti-drug strategy. Essential to effective
interdiction and federal drug enforcement are: coordination and
cooperation among the agencies, reliable and timely strategic, tactical,
operational intelligence, effective laws, and adequate resources.

The National Drug Policy Board

Strong leadership to coordinate a national narcotics control strategy
is vital to our nation's future. Therefore, I was pleased to note that the
Administration will attempt to centralize drug control policy—both supply
and demand—in one Cabinet level board, the National Drug Policy
Board. I sincerely hope that this new policy board will be able to provide the necessary leadership.

I am concerned, however, that this new board will not provide the
answer to two questions that many of us in Congress are asking: Who
is in charge of federal drug abuse policy? Who will determine the Administration's drug-related budgetary priorities? I hope that Mr. Stephen
Trott* will be able to provide us answers to our concerns about leadership and cooperation.

---

*Editor's note: Stephen Trott's biography appears on page 80 of
Reading 10.

Illustration by Craig MacIntosh. Reprinted by permission of *Star Tribune, Newspaper of the Twin Cities.*

Our enforcement and interdiction efforts must be more than a matter of luck or accident. This requires reliable intelligence about broad trends in order to develop policies and plans, tactical information to detect and identify targets, and operational intelligence to support the investigative and prosecutorial processes.

Cooperation Necessary in the War Against Drugs

The Anti-Drug Abuse Act of 1986 provided a variety of resources, equipment, and facilities to enhance our drug-related intelligence capacity. For example, the Coast Guard and Customs Service have each been provided with two E-2C's, radar-equipped aircraft. Customs has been authorized to establish command, control, communications, and intelligence centers (C3-I's) to provide tactical coordination for interdiction efforts. Additional aerostats are authorized for the southwest border and the Bahamas; this will increase radar detection capabilities.

To be effective, the information gathered must be used; it must be shared. Coordination is critical. This is not the place for turf battles, misplaced agency loyalty, or false bravado. I hope we will be able to learn not only about the progress that has been made in deploying the new equipment, but of more effective coordination and increased cooperation among the agencies involved in interdiction and enforcement.

Effective laws and adequate resources are necessary to ensure that our borders are securely fortified. The Anti-Drug Abuse Act addressed both of these areas. The legislation provided the personnel and equipment resources necessary to meet current needs. Changes in our federal criminal statutes were enacted to ensure more effective drug law enforcement.

Budget Cuts Will Not Help

We in the Congress demonstrated our commitment to federal drug enforcement and interdiction when we passed the Anti-Drug Abuse Act of 1986. Although the President's proposed 1988 budget makes fewer cuts in these areas than it does in drug abuse education, prevention, treatment, and state and local drug enforcement assistance programs, reductions in significant provisions are made.

For example, their 1988 proposal reduces the Customs Service by approximately 1,998 positions. Moreover, the 1988 request of $86 million for the Customs Air program, a critical link in our interdiction effort, is half of the 1987 funding level of $171 million. These proposals jeopardize the expansion of Customs drug inspections at our borders, the development of facilities to coordinate interdiction activities effectively, the deployment of upgraded radar on drug surveillance aircraft, and the operation of aircraft to track marine drug smugglers.

The 1988 request for federal drug enforcement spending is also lower than the 1987 level because approximately $350 million appropriated for capital purchases in 1987 is not repeated in the 1988 budget.

The 1988 budget does include about $70 million in increases for federal drug law enforcement. This includes $32 million and 108 positions for the Drug Enforcement Administration, $2.4 million and 85 positions for the Federal Bureau of Investigation, $21.4 million and 417 positions for the United States Attorneys, and $8.5 million and 112 positions for the U.S. Marshals Service. I support these increases in the Justice Department's drug enforcement programs, but these increases in no way alleviate the responsibility to fund those activities Congress authorized in the Anti-Drug Abuse Act.

12

CONTROLLING
THE DRUG EPIDEMIC

GROWING SUCCESS
IN THE NARCOTICS
INTERDICTION PROGRAM

John C. Whitehead

John Whitehead presented the following testimony in his capacity as Deputy Secretary of State. Mr. Whitehead testified before a subcommittee of the Senate Committee on Appropriations and discussed the administration's international narcotics control programs and policies.

Points to Consider:

1. Compare and contrast the number of governments engaged in eradication programs in 1981 and 1985. Why do you think these numbers changed?
2. Describe some of the eradication efforts taking place in foreign countries.
3. In what ways are the United States and Mexico working together to control the drug problem?
4. How does the U.S. fund narcotic control objectives throughout the world?

Excerpted from testimony of John C. Whitehead before the Subcommittee on Foreign Operations of the Senate Committee on Appropriations, August 14, 1986.

Continued and increased pressure has to be applied at all points of the chain: through crop control; through increased seizure of both drug products and financial assets; through intensified investigation and prosecution of traffickers; and through effective treatment and prevention of drug abuse.

International Narcotics Control

Let there be no mistake that this administration is fully committed to stopping the flow of illicit narcotics into our country. The danger of narcotics to our society and to the very fabric of our society cannot be a subject of partisan debate. We are grateful for the support this committee has provided for the administration's efforts in the past, and I am confident we can count on your continued support for the future.

International narcotics control is central to the pursuit of our foreign policy objectives. We have and will continue to use every opportunity to convey the message to our friends in the international community on the need for greater effort in controlling narcotics traffic. . . .

Universal Threat from Illegal Drug Traffic

The most effective tool we have in this effort is the growing realization among foreign governments that narcotics trafficking is not just an American problem, but a universal threat. The efforts of the First Lady and our high-level attention to this problem are already paying dividends. Countries in which narcotics are produced or which are part of the international trafficking pattern now recognize the unacceptably high risk that narcotics pose to their own societies.

These risks range from increases in violent crime to national security threats by narco-terrorist groups. The international community is finally recognizing the challenge we all face. That is the first and most important step in winning the battle.

Nevertheless, there remains a large and unacceptable gap between perception and effective action. We expect more concrete measures from our friends and are prepared to encourage and support them. The situation remains serious.

U.S. Foreign Policy Objectives

From the foreign policy perspective, our highest priority is to reduce production. We are moving closer to our objective of having effective eradication programs in all key producing countries. In 1981, only two governments were engaged in eradication programs. By 1985, the list had grown to 14. As a result, marijuana production is today declining

---

THE REAGAN RECORD ON DRUG INTERDICTION

Interdiction focuses on detecting, intercepting, and apprehending shipments of illegal drugs as they move into the U.S. by air, land, or sea. The task is difficult because ours is an open society with open borders. Nonetheless, the U.S. Coast Guard, the Customs Service, and the Immigration and Naturalization Service, supported by the Department of Defense, annually seize millions of pounds of illegal drugs.

In fiscal year 1987 alone, federal agents interdicted and seized approximately 639 pounds of heroin; a record 92,000 pounds of cocaine; and an estimated two million pounds of marijuana.

The White House, Office of the Press Secretary, May 18, 1988

---

in Colombia, Jamaica, and other countries in Latin America and the Caribbean. We expect that trend to continue.

Current Colombian experiments to identify environmentally safe herbicides which can be reproduced on a large scale could provide a new tool for eradicating coca plants. The recent dramatic demonstration of the renewed commitment of the Bolivian government to narcotics control has resulted in the price of the coca leaf falling to an all-time low. I met with President Paz Estenssoro and his senior officials in La Paz this spring and know directly of their concerns and their need for support. . . .

Several countries are working hard to contain the problem. Ecuador, which collaborated with Colombia on a joint coca eradication effort along their common border, is intensifying both its eradication and interdiction efforts for 1986. Brazil, with U.S. assistance, initiated operations to destroy both coca and marijuana, as well as important seizure campaigns, while also expanding its efforts to interdict shipments of precursor chemicals used in cocaine refining.

Like Colombia, Panama and Belize conducted aerial eradication programs, using herbicides, in 1985 and 1986. Following the spraying this spring, Panamanian production of marijuana dropped sharply enough that authorities think aerial spraying is no longer needed. Jamaica initiated a long-needed manual eradication campaign to destroy both spring and fall marijuana crops in 1985, resulting in gains that have been confirmed by aerial surveys. Brazil, Costa Rica, Guatemala, and other governments have also destroyed marijuana plantations. . . .

Bolivia must complete the planning for both the voluntary and involuntary phases of its eradication campaign, and bring a substantial portion of its illicit coca acreage under control, enforced by eradication

Cartoon by Doug MacGregor. Copyright 1988, *USA Today*. Reprinted with permission.

where necessary, enhanced by alternative development opportunities where appropriate. The government recognizes that continued assistance is dependent in part on achieving the eradication targets in the new agreement now being negotiated with the United States.

The killings and lawlessness in Peru's Upper Huallaga Valley continue, proving again that narcotics control and the battle against terrorism must both share a high priority with the government of Peru. Economic and military assistance to Peru in 1987 are dependent in part on the development and implementation of a comprehensive strategy for coca control.

The strategic task in 1986 and 1987 is to extend the coca eradication campaign into additional growing areas of the Upper Huallaga Valley. Coca eradication in the Valley doubled in 1985, but the new areas are quite inaccessible and the pace of manual eradication may be difficult to sustain. . . .

In Southeast Asia, Burma now has the opportunity, with production down in 1985 and a major eradication program having been successfully undertaken in the first quarter of 1986, to reduce the world's largest production of illicit opium. In Thailand, the new eradication program is being expanded. These governments must enhance their efforts to seize control of the border from traffickers, to destroy heroin laboratories, and to interdict shipments of both precursor chemicals and finished opium products. . . .

Pakistan and neighboring nations must also find ways of curbing the flow of opium products out of Afghanistan and suppressing the numerous heroin labs which operate along the Afghan-Pakistan border. Viable approaches have not been found to Iran or to Laos, and reports on increased opium production in the latter are of renewed concern, particularly given success elsewhere in the Golden Triangle. . . .

U.S./Mexico Drug Program

The United States and Mexico have reiterated their unrestricted cooperation and assistance in rejuvenating a control program.

We have emphasized the high priority we attach to reducing the flow of heroin and marijuana from Mexico. . . . In September, the United States and Mexico will collaborate in an intensive spraying program of opium poppy in the infamous tristate area. Mexico has agreed to let us bring in six turboflush aircraft and combine them with three of their high-spraying capacity Bell 212 helicopters in an effort to eliminate 70 percent or more of the fall poppy crop before it is harvested.

We have assisted the Mexicans in improving this program in 1986, including refinements in the spraying process. Together with the verification program, in which DEA agents ride with Mexican officials to confirm fields destroyed, these improvements bode well for restoring the effectiveness of this once heralded program.

However, we have other problems: The level of effectiveness in seizures, arrests, and prosecutions has never been as good as in the eradication program. We seek a strong, across-the-board effort at improving enforcement.

Administration Request for Antidrug Funding

The tools and resources provided by Congress are critical assets supporting our diplomatic efforts. The administration's fiscal year 1987 budget request for $65.4 million for international narcotics control programs includes a substantial increase in funds for eradication. We also have requested more funds for enforcement efforts, supporting crop reduction activities. Seventy-three percent of available funding is dedicated to these very efforts.

We urge the committee to appropriate the full amount. We also have used economic assistance funds administered by the Agency for International Development (AID) in direct and indirect support of our narcotic control objectives. In Peru, Bolivia, and Pakistan, for example, the disbursement of development assistance funds is tied to achieving specific narcotic control objectives in target areas.

In Thailand, AID and International Narcotics Matters of the Department of State (INM) are funding a project in which entire villages must agree to keep farming areas free of poppy. This program is going well with the support of the Thai army's aggressive new eradication program.

We still have a long way to go. I would not minimize the obstacles, but I am heartened by what I believe are clearly positive trends. I believe that our friends recognize the need to eliminate this scourge. They know that we mean business. Continued and increased pressure has to be applied at all points of the chain: through crop control; through increased seizure of both drug products and financial assets; through intensified investigation and prosecution of traffickers, and through effective treatment and prevention of drug abuse.

CONTROLLING
THE DRUG EPIDEMIC

THE TOTAL FAILURE
OF INTERDICTION

Office of Technology Assessment

The Office of Technology Assessment (OTA) was created in 1972 as an analytical arm of Congress. OTA's basic function is to help legislative policymakers anticipate and plan for the consequences of technological changes and to examine the many ways in which technology affects people's lives. OTA provides Congress with independent and timely information about the potential effects of technological applications.

Points to Consider:

1. What kind of profit do drug smugglers realize from the sale of illegal drugs?
2. Which agencies have primary responsibility for drug interdiction?
3. Summarize the OTA's key findings regarding U.S. drug interdiction efforts.
4. How could interdiction efforts be improved?

U.S. Congress, Office of Technology Assessment, *The Border War on Drugs,* OTA-O-336 (Washington, D.C.: U.S. Government Printing Office, March 1987).

Despite increasing federal expenditures for interdiction, illegal drug imports appear to be increasing.

Despite a doubling of federal expenditures on interdiction over the past five years, the quantity of drugs smuggled into the United States is greater than ever. Illegal imports of cocaine, the drug now of intense national concern, have about doubled since 1981, supplying a growing number of users at prices that have fallen as the supply has increased.

Illegal Drugs: A Big Problem

The challenge faced by drug enforcement agencies is formidable. The Office of Technology Assessment (OTA) estimates that U.S. retail sales of marijuana, cocaine, and heroin totaled about $50 billion in 1985. A survey taken at that time indicated that 18.2 million Americans used marijuana once or more a month and 5.8 million were monthly users of cocaine. Overall, 10 percent of the population over age 12 were found to be monthly users of marijuana and 3 percent were monthly users of cocaine. Other data indicate that 500,000 persons in this country use heroin regularly.[1]

The large market, coupled with the huge profits to be made by transporting drugs from foreign suppliers to domestic wholesalers, fuels this illegal traffic. OTA estimates that the mark-up between foreign and domestic wholesale prices is on the order to 20 to 30 times for marijuana, 4 to 5 for cocaine, and 30 to 40 for heroin. In 1985, the value added to the product through smuggling was roughly $6 billion for mari-

---

[1] The number of regular marijuana users and heroin addicts has been reported in the annual Narcotics Intelligence Estimate published by the Drug Enforcement Administration (DEA) and in the most recent (June 1986) DEA Special Report, "Worldwide Drug Assessment." Estimates of heroin addicts are based on a 1981 survey. Marijuana usage is based on 1982 and 1985 National Institute of Drug Abuse (NIDA) "Household Surveys." The 1985 National Household Survey on Drug Abuse published by NIDA puts the number of regular cocaine users at about 5,800,000. Total U.S. consumption of cocaine appears to have increased 20 to 30 percent from 1982 to 1986. Some researchers believe that the number of users may not be growing as much as the incidence of very heavy usage. In addition, the 1985 University of Michigan survey of high school students states that cocaine use by high school seniors was at an all-time high (17 percent have tried cocaine), and that this would indicate increased use among that group in the future.

juana, $1.6 billion for cocaine, and $1 billion for heroin. Of this, perhaps 90 percent (over $7 billion) was realized as profit by drug smugglers.

The drug traffic moves by a great variety of transport modes and routes to reach the United States. Most imported marijuana comes either by sea in private vessels or by land across the Mexican border, but private aircraft and commercial transport are also used. Cocaine is smuggled across all three coasts and the Mexican border, with about half the traffic carried in private aircraft and a large share of the remainder in private vessels. The amount of cocaine smuggled through ports of entry appears to be increasing. The heroin produced in Southeast and Southwest Asia is primarily carried by airline passengers through ports of entry or hidden in cargo or mail. An increasing amount of Mexican heroin enters across the land border. Smugglers show great ingenuity in devising methods of entry. When interdiction efforts restrict a particular mode of transport or route, drug traffickers quickly shift to alternatives. As a result, the nation's long and highly permeable borders are being assaulted by an illegal traffic that uses all conceivable means of transport and concealment.

United States Interdiction Efforts

The agencies with primary responsibility for drug interdiction are the Customs Service and the Coast Guard. The Customs Service is charged with combating smuggling by private aircraft, by private vessels in near-shore waters, and by all modes at ports of entry. The Coast Guard shares responsibility with Customs for interdiction of sea-borne drug traffic near shore and conducts patrols along the entire U.S. coastline and in the open ocean, focusing on the Gulf of Mexico and the Caribbean Sea. Along the Mexican border between ports of entry, the Border Patrol of the Immigration and Naturalization Service exercises enforce-

ment effort as an adjunct to its primary mission of preventing illegal immigration.

These front-line agencies, supported by numerous other federal agencies, have seized increasing quantities of drugs over the past five years. In fiscal year 1986, almost $800 million was expended by the federal government in this effort. Despite these efforts only a small percentage of drugs are being seized, and the flow of drugs into this country has not yet been stemmed. (Seizure rates vary according to the particular drug, the season of the year, locale, and mode of transport.)

The Anti-Drug Abuse Act of 1986 (Public Law 99-570) affirms the role of interdiction as an important element in drug law enforcement. The act authorizes a substantial increase in funding for interdiction resources and personnel and greater use of military assets. It also sets the stage for resolving some of the fragmentation in organization and responsibilities for drug interdiction (e.g., between Coast Guard and Customs). It establishes mechanisms for allocating new military equipment and the requirement for legislative proposals from the President by mid-1987 to reorganize executive branch efforts to combat drug trafficking and abuse.

The goal of the nation's overall anti-drug abuse program is to reduce the number of users and prevent others from becoming users. The national strategy includes many elements of both supply and demand reduction. Interdiction is only one element of supply reduction, which also includes investigation and prosecution, and international narcotics control. While many debate the relative merits of each of these elements, most agree that some level of effort in each is necessary.

101

Central to the success of future drug interdiction efforts are the technologies employed to detect, intercept, and capture smugglers. This study investigates the availability, use, and performance of the technologies now used for this and others that could contribute to the nation's effort to prevent illegal drug traffic. Understanding the present contribution and potential improvement of these technologies involves not only examining the technologies themselves, but also the organizations that use these systems and the enforcement strategies they employ.

Key Findings

1. Despite increasing federal expenditures for interdiction, illegal drug imports appear to be increasing. **There is no clear correlation between the level of expenditures or effort devoted to interdiction and the long-term availability of illegally imported drugs in the domestic market.** However, given the profitability of drug smuggling, a worldwide glut of drugs, and the view that the United States is the favored market for drugs, interdiction alone will probably never result in more than a short-term or relatively small reduction in drug availability.

2. OTA found the federal agencies charged with the responsibility of drug interdiction to be staffed by dedicated and vigorous personnel who demonstrate courage and imagination in carrying out their responsibilities. For the most part, however, they have had to operate with very limited technological resources. **The size, scope, and diversity of the smuggling challenge is enormous compared to the human and equipment resources that front-line enforcement agencies can bring to bear.**

3. **Data on drug smuggling, the trafficking system, and interdiction activities are inadequate for effective planning and management.** Such data are needed to make informed selection of best strategies, to allocate enforcement resources, and to guide the design and management of interdiction programs. Measures of effectiveness for interdiction are difficult to define precisely. The numbers and quantities of drug seizures are difficult to interpret without good knowledge about smuggling attempts. Often, intelligence reports provide the best information on the effect of interdiction efforts on smuggling activity.

4. **Responsibilities of the federal drug interdiction agencies are fragmented and overlapping.** The lack of a suitable institutional framework is a major impediment to the adoption and effective use of technologies, particularly command and control systems that could offer significant benefits. With the exception of special intensive operations, problems with interagency coordination and

cooperation occur, and no central authority addresses important strategic questions on priorities and resource allocation.

5. Lack of an overall direction that would establish a comprehensive approach to planning and operations, limits the effectiveness of interdiction programs. Improved direction could enable:
—enforcement resources to be allocated to the highest priority problems;
—the various agencies to design and carry out more effective coordinated interdiction strategies; and
—the effectiveness of interdiction programs to be evaluated.

6. **The value of intelligence is very high for all aspects of drug interdiction.** In particular, good tactical intelligence can mean a large increase in ability to identify smuggling attempts. In certain areas, intelligence gathering is limited by inadequate resources and an ineffective network. Needed information cannot be gathered and delivered to the users in a timely fashion. Classified intelligence, even if valuable to interdiction efforts, is not often or easily used because of concerns about revealing sources and methods during court proceedings.

7. Over the past two years many new technologies, ranging from remote sensors to pursuit aircraft and patrol boats, have been introduced into federal drug interdiction programs. These technologies have, for the most part, enhanced federal capabilities. However, the technologies are just now becoming operational and evaluations of their overall effectiveness cannot be made without more experience and a directed effort to collect relevant data for evaluation.

8. **No single technology has been identified that by its addition would solve the nation's overall drug interdiction problem.** But there are many opportunities for individual technologies to make incremental contributions to specific federal interdiction efforts. Realizing these opportunities may require development of new technologies or procurement of increased numbers of existing technologies. However, most technological improvements, by themselves, may have only a temporary benefit because, based on the record, the drug traffickers will take rapid and usually successful actions to neutralize the effectiveness of new interdiction techniques.

9. **There is a serious lack of support for research, development, testing, and evaluation of new or transferred technologies within all of the drug interdiction agencies.** Opportunities exist within other federal agencies (especially the national laboratories and Department of Defense (DOD) laboratories) to provide some of the needed capabilities. . . .

OTA Suggestions for Improvement

This OTA assessment of interdiction technologies suggests a range of options that could be employed by the federal agencies in an effort to improve the effectiveness of future operations, increase success within their operational strategies, and make more efficient use of resources. These options are listed below:

- The principal interdiction agencies, under the direction of the National Drug Enforcement Policy Board, the National Narcotics Border Interdiction System, or another central authority, could prepare a coordinated long-range plan for deployment of interdiction resources and technologies to apply pressure on major smuggling modes at ports of entry and air, marine, and land borders. This would entail matching resources to the present threat and developing a system to assure that consistent monitoring of trafficking is fed into the planning process. The plan could include networks for intelligence and surveillance data as well as designated commands for specific arenas. OTA has noted throughout its report deficiencies in information and command networks and has stressed centralized planning.

- Establish a system and standards common to all agencies which would be used to evaluate deterrent capabilities and the effectiveness of technologies and techniques used for interdiction. The system would need to include specified data to be collected, standards for measuring detection and apprehension rates, consistent costing methods, and procedures for using the most appropriate data to evaluate systems or operations.

- For the port of entry interdiction problem, the Customs Service or another agency could establish a substantial research and development (R&D) program to develop more effective detection technologies. OTA has found that there is some promise of technological advancement in this area, but R&D efforts are too small to conduct needed work. Existing national laboratories could provide the technical base for a major R&D effort.

- For illegal border entry interdiction (air, marine, and land), a cooperative agency group could design a border surveillance-detection network for smuggler traffic. OTA has found that sufficient technologies (mostly military) are available to address this problem, but that a design for deployment is lacking.

CONTROLLING
THE DRUG EPIDEMIC

ERADICATING DRUGS
IN PRODUCER NATIONS:
THE POINT

James Mills

At the time he wrote this article, James Mills had spent the last six years working on a then-recently published book about the international narcotics industry.

Points to Consider:

1. What are the benefits of eradication?
2. Explain why the United States government and foreign countries avoid eradication.
3. Which country has the highest per capita addiction rate in the world? How many addicts does the country have?
4. Why are drug traffickers laughing at the war on drugs?

Not only is eradication the only remedy that has worked, it is also the only approach that directly attacks the fundamental problem—removing drugs.

What do the traffickers themselves think of all this drug hysteria—President Reagan's urinalysis, the first blockade of New York harbor since the War of 1812, proposals to seal the Mexican border with a 2,000-mile cocaine curtain?

In a fortified mansion in Bankok, in a Mexico City prison, in homes, hotel rooms and restaurants on four continents, I have spoken to a few of the men who run the international narcotics industry, and I am certain their reaction to the war on drugs is the same today as when I met them. They are laughing.

Getting to the Cause of the Drug Problem

With each desperate new response to the drug dilemma, we move further and further from the real solution and give the narcotics tycoons every reason to celebrate.

When an intelligent person has a problem, he first examines the problem, breaks it into its components, tries to find the fundamental cause (as opposed to symptoms masquerading as causes), and then attacks that cause. He also asks himself what attacks have been made on the problem in the past, and which, if any, of those attacks have had success.

Clearly, the cause of the drug problem is drugs. If drugs had never existed there could be no drug problem.

Apparent solution: Remove drugs. Without the presence of drugs, there would be no need for programs to interdict drugs, arrest drug dealers, seize drug profits, treat drug addicts, or test potential drug users.

What attacks have been launched against the drug problem in the past? They include: interdiction, law enforcement, penalties, treatment, denying profits, eradication.

Which of these, if any, have worked? Only one: eradication.

Using Eradication to Fight Drugs

It worked in Turkey, and it worked, more recently and temporarily, in Mexico. None of the others has ever worked, to any significant degree, anywhere at any time.

Doesn't common sense tell us that before we throw billions of dollars and immense effort at other recommended attacks on the problem, we should fully exhaust attempts at eradication, the only remedy that has ever worked?

106

Not only is eradication the only remedy that has worked, it is also the only approach that directly attacks the fundamental problem—removing drugs.

Eradication also happens, fortunately, to be the cheapest and easiest approach.

Ninety-five percent of the world's cocaine, for example, originates in only two countries, Peru and Bolivia. They have a combined population approximately equal to that of California. They are impoverished and desperately in need of aid. Surely it would be relatively easy to encourage—and, if necessary to force—those countries to stop growing coca.

A few weeks ago, President Victor Paz Estenssoro of Bolivia, asking for $100 million a year in antidrug funds from the United States, was quoted as saying: "If we are going to tell the peasants not to grow coca, we have to have alternatives. Without an all-weather highway, they can't market rice, coffee, oranges, and other legal crops they could substitute for coca."

I first heard those words—virtually verbatim—about a decade ago from Thailand officials. The Thais got the money they requested, they got their crop-substitution programs, and they got their highway.

Today, the money is gone, crop substitution is still in the "demonstration" stage, poppy acreage is vastly increased and the highway has been used to transport opium and morphine base.

It is also argued that if we eradicate in one country, growers will simply shift to another. This ignores the fact that there are only a limited number of locations with the agricultural and climatic conditions necessary for the growth of coca and poppies.

Cartoon by David Seavey. Copyright 1986, *USA Today*. Reprinted with permission.

And once the full power of the United States comes down on Peru and Bolivia, forcing eradication, surely other countries will see the handwriting on the wall. Will they imagine that they can succeed where Peru and Bolivia failed? Would not the United States be as capable of coercing those countries into eradication as it was Peru and Bolivia?

And isn't there something fundamentally unsound, and craven, about the other-countries-will-step-in argument? Is it wise not to attack one enemy for fear that others might then appear?

Why Is Eradication Rarely Used?

After having observed the international drug scene for 20 years, I am convinced that eradication is the only thing that will work, and that it would work quite easily. If Reagan dug in his heels and became obsessive about eradication, he could reduce the availability of cocaine by 50 percent in six months, and by 80 percent in a year. Heroin could be similarly reduced, though over a longer period of time.

Why, then, is eradication always at the bottom of every politician's list of things to do? I think because it's the least politically attractive recommendation.

Surely, it is no accident that the present furor over drugs (sparked only in part by the emergence of crack) precedes the November elections by three months. (Reagan declared his war on drugs 19 days before the 1982 elections.) Politicians appear to believe that workers are interested only in what is nearest to them. So we get domestic solutions: interdiction, testing, and enforcement. Eradication—a big word that happens in distant lands—isn't so viscerally appealing as capital punishment for pushers.

We have to stop wanting to appear as if we are doing something— and do something. There is no end to the good you can accomplish if you don't care who gets the credit. Eradication could make all other approaches, from interdiction to testing, irrelevant.

Complaints from Foreign Countries

Both Peru and Bolivia complain that eradication of coca plants would unduly upset peasants who earn their living from coca. But when members of the Senate Select Committee on Narcotics Abuse and Control visited Peru and Bolivia in 1983 they found that many, if not most, of the coca-growing campesinos had until recently been growing legitimate food crops.

Only when the campesinos abandoned food crops for the more lucrative coca plants did both those countries have to be fed by emergency international relief programs.

Bolivia further claims that since campesinos represent 60 percent of the electorate, their disfavor could topple the government. Well, so what—compared to the alternative of continuing cocaine abuse? Bolivian governments have been collapsing regularly for the past 30 years, and will no doubt continue to collapse with or without the eradication of coca fields.

Note that Thailand has offered the peasant-will-starve argument for some 15 years, while its poppy acreage has grown and grown.

Turkey said the same thing (it had 300,000 farmers growing poppies)—until President Richard Nixon gave the Turkish government money for the farmers who were put out of the opium business in the early 1970's. Most of the money went into the pockets of corrupt officials. Still, there were no reports of mass starvation in Turkey.

We Need a World War on Drugs

I might also add that drugs are not exclusively an American problem. The war must be a world war—not only in the sense that producing countries are our enemies, but in the sense that other victim countries are, or should be, our allies.

We do not have the highest per capita addiction rate in the world. (Colombia is said to have three million addicts, which is one in nine citizens—almost unbelievable.) Many countries in Asia, Latin America, and Europe have large and growing drug problems. They should be as eager as we to see to it that producing countries get out of the dope business.

Last year, 23 Americans died in terrorist attacks, and we bombed Libya. If the world's coca fields were in Libya, instead of in Peru and Bolivia, Reagan would know what to do, and we would not have a cocaine problem today.

By concentrating the bulk of its efforts on domestic approaches, our government keeps the heat off the leaders of the international narcotics industry, men whose supply, production, and management teams are overseas.

So the traffickers are laughing. They know how to solve the drug problem. The war on drugs is the best thing that ever happened to them.

CONTROLLING
THE DRUG EPIDEMIC

ERADICATING DRUGS
IN PRODUCER NATIONS:
THE COUNTERPOINT

Penny Lernoux

Penny Lernoux wrote this article in her capacity as Latin American affairs writer for the National Catholic Reporter, *a liberal, independent Catholic newsweekly.*

Points to Consider:

1. Does the author believe eradication will work? Why or why not?
2. Explain why the United States blames the drug problem on Latin America.
3. What happens to U.S. aid for antidrug programs in Latin America?
4. How would Latin Americans confront the drug problem?

Penny Lernoux, "Lucrative South American Drug Trade High on U.S. Consumers," *National Catholic Reporter,* March 25, 1988, pp. 1, 18. Reprinted by permission of the *National Catholic Reporter,* P.O. Box 419281, Kansas City, MO. 64141.

So long as Americans are willing to spend millions of dollars annually on cocaine, poor peasants will grow coca leaves and rich traffickers will buy governments.

I've had on my desk since last year pictures of a corpse of a 15 year-old Bolivian boy who died in a drug rehabilitation center operated by Bolivia's U.S.-financed anti-narcotics police. The documents also include a detailed description of the murder of a 16-year-old in the same center. But the papers got pushed to the bottom of a pile of clippings on the murders of priests, judges, journalists, and government officials who were killed in Colombia by the same sickness.

Supplying the U.S. Drug Market

There are thousands of such cases in the drug-producing countries—so many that I've given up trying to keep track of more than a few. The rest go into a filing cabinet that I think of as the drug morgue—the victims of a narcotics traffic that feeds the habits of millions of U.S. consumers. Most were innocent bystanders who happened to be standing on a street corner when the narcos' paid assassins machine-gunned everyone in sight, or were murdered because they spoke out against the traffickers. Some were well-known—among the victims in Colombia were the justice minister and the attorney general—but most were poor and anonymous, like the 15-year-old Bolivian.

The innocent blood daily shed to supply the U.S. drug market is not often discussed by the U.S. media, which follows Washington's line in claiming it is all the fault of the Latin American countries that produce cocaine and marijuana. If the Latin American governments would just wipe out the producers, by dropping toxic chemicals on tens of thousands of peasants, there would be no supply, goes the argument. But poisoning peasants and the environment will not stop the supply. Much of the marijuana consumed in the United States is now grown locally, and so long as Americans are willing to spend billions of dollars annually on cocaine, poor peasants will grow coca leaves and rich traffickers will buy governments.

Neither the Republicans nor the Democrats are willing to address the root of the problem in the United States, because it is political dynamite, as a former congressman said. Millions of voters are drug consumers; millions more oppose drug use. Politicians therefore avoid the controversial issue by blaming the Latin Americans.

Financial Support for Antidrug Programs

Under Ronald Reagan the policy has been to provide some financial support for antidrug programs in Latin America and to pressure governments to comply by threatening to cut off all aid, as has occurred

112

LITTLE PROGRESS IN ERADICATION

The government of Colombia is paralyzed in its efforts to re-spond effectively to the drug trafficking organizations.

Fear and intimidation tactics have rendered the Colombian criminal justice system unable to prosecute major drug traffickers in civilian courts. Over 30 judges have been assassinated. The wives and children of judges, and public officials have also been the targets of narco-terrorist attacks. . . .

There was little progress on the drug enforcement and eradica-tion effort in Colombia in 1986. Although the marijuana eradication campaign destroyed 9,700 hectares in 1986, coca eradication con-tinues to be nonexistent.

Moreover, since January 1, 1987, only four cocaine processing labs had been destroyed, although many more have been iden-tified. Arrests of major drug traffickers are rarely made.

Excerpted from a report of the House of Representatives Select Committee on Narcotics Abuse and Control, March 16-17, 1987

with Bolivia. But U.S. aid is a pittance compared to the billions of dollars in drug profits, and often the money goes to police forces that are themselves involved in the traffic.

In Bolivia, for example, the U.S. antidrug commitment last year was $14 million, compared to over $1 billion from the drug trade. And Washington slashed nearly $9 million from the total when the Bolivian government could not fulfill a commitment to destroy 135,000 acres of coca plants, largely because of the organized protests of some 40,000 peasants who depend on coca growing for a living. Meanwhile, the supposedly incorruptible antidrug police, the Mobile Rural Patrol Unit, which was created and trained by the U.S. Drug Enforcement Ad-ministration and the U.S. Army, has become notorious for drug corrup-tion and the abuse of peasants.

U.S. and Bolivian officials have admitted that the Leopards, as the antidrug police are popularly known, routinely accept bribes, and in one case—the rehabilitation center where the Bolivian teenagers died—witnesses testified that youths imprisoned in the center were used as labor in a coca paste operation. . . .

We Need More Public Education

Parents in the United States suffer greatly when their children are snared by the drug culture, but I wonder if they realize that the children

in these poor Latin American countries suffer at least as much, and often more.

None of the governments of the producing countries has the money or means to deal with the challenge individually, and the dribble of U.S. aid has as much impact as a gnat on an elephant. As the Latin Americans have repeatedly stated, the only way to confront the problem is through collective action, the emphasis being on public education instead of police seizures that net a few second-level traffickers and a few kilos of cocaine but have no impact on supply and demand.

A good way to start such action would be to get some attention on the issue during the U.S. presidential campaign. I suppose I shouldn't be surprised, but I find it dismaying that none of the major candidates has addressed—or been asked to address—a question of life-and-death importance to so many people in our hemisphere.

16

CONTROLLING
THE DRUG EPIDEMIC

USING THE MILITARY
IN THE WAR ON DRUGS:
POINTS AND COUNTERPOINTS

USA Today vs. Barbara Reynolds

*The following counterpoints were excerpted from the opinion page of
USA Today, a national daily newspaper. The point is the opinion of
USA Today; Barbara Reynolds wrote the counterpoint in her capacity
as an editor and member of the USA Today editorial board.*

Points to Consider:

1. Why do the authors of the point argue that using the military would
   not help in the war on drugs?
2. What suggestions do the authors of the point offer as options to
   military involvement?
3. How does Barbara Reynolds suggest we deal with the drug
   problem?
4. Do you agree with the point or counterpoint? Why?

THE POINT—by *USA Today*

The USA is being overwhelmed—by drugs.

From Mexico and the Bahamas. From Panama and Haiti. From throughout the Caribbean, the Medellin drug cartel of Colombia and other drug lords ship more than 100 tons of cocaine across our borders each year.

Lethal Imports

When those lethal imports finally land, they explode in crime and death.

In one borough of New York City alone, drug gangs have slain more than 500 people. And thugs executed a rookie cop—Edward Byrne— who was guarding a witness in a drug case.

Eight people aboard the Continental Express commuter jet that crashed in Durango, Colo., Jan. 19 may have been victims of drug abuse. Traces of cocaine were found in blood and urine samples of the plane's pilot.

Across the USA, thousands of children live in broken homes or suffer abuse because of drugs. Millions of us are victims of drug-related crimes.

The Military Will Not Win War on Drugs

Such tragedies outrage us. And we are frustrated when we see so few gains in our war against drugs.

Federal spending in the drug war has climbed from $861 million in 1981 to $3 billion this year. U.S. cocaine seizures have gone up from 4,000 pounds in 1981 to 80,000 pounds last year. Arrests have increased from 13,000 to 21,000.

Yet, the amount of cocaine pouring across our borders has doubled. Six million of us now abuse cocaine each month. And violence abounds.

No wonder people want to lash out at countries that harbor drug lords who export death. But it would be foolish for us to use the military to chase them, as some suggest.

We tried that in Bolivia in 1986. Our soldiers burned coca crops and destroyed labs there only to see new labs open and new fields sown after they left.

We can't wage war in Latin America. It would violate international law. It would waste time and money.

But there are some things we can do.

Other Options Are Available

We can cut aid and trade to governments, such as Panama's, where high officials are implicated in drug crimes. We can use diplomacy to get nations, such as Mexico, to clean up widespread corruption that permits drug running. We can provide aid to countries, such as Colombia, where drug thugs threaten leaders with murder. We can provide advice and equipment to governments whose leaders sincerely want to wage war on drugs.

And we can provide the Customs Service and the Coast Guard the manpower and money they need to guard our borders.

But we don't need to call up the military or give up the fight by legalizing drugs.

Instead, we must attack the enemy within. We must teach our children about drug dangers. We must expand our treatment programs for drug abusers. We must increase prison space to put away drug dealers.

We can win the war against drugs. But to do so, we must win the battle at home.

THE COUNTERPOINT—by Barbara Reynolds

For all the wrong reasons, U.S. military or CIA forces have mined, undermined, and invaded such nations as Vietnam, Nicaragua and Grenada, the tiny isle of nutmeg.

But now, when there are sound reasons—a growing U.S. body count, our communities under siege and our minds being blown—we are reluctant to use the military to fight back.

Call Out the Troops

Not only should we send out troops into Latin America to put down the murderous drug cartels—the source of our enemy within—we should also call out the National Guard to protect innocent lives in the USA and return communities to the decent citizens who live there.

The $8 billion Colombian drug cartel has the potential to accomplish what communism could never do—destroy us from the inside.

Cartoon by David Seavey. Copyright 1988, *USA Today.* Reprinted with permission.

More than 10 percent of us regularly use drugs. Drugs cost employers more than $33 billion each year in lost productivity, and a recent 12-city study showed 53 percent to 79 percent of all men arrested for serious crimes last year were drug users.

Shattering Our Way of Life

As a city dweller in the nation's capital—home of the commander in chief of the world's most powerful military force—I see illegal drug use tragically shattering our way of life, hanging like a shroud over our children's future.

For example, conversation stops as the drug death toll is updated on the evening news. So far this year, 67 percent of the city's 54 homicides have been due to local drug war, much of it waged by Jamaican thugs who are out-gunning and overrunning local police.

Drugs and death have become a part of the inner-city school curriculum, where youths who in days past talked of sock hops and slumber parties are now trading stories of mothers and fathers sharing crack with their children, teachers getting high with their students, and the tears shed at the most recent funeral.

Libertarians would argue that military force would be too excessive and troops patrolling endangered streets at home would destroy hard-won constitutional freedoms.

More moderate weapons, however, are not working.

Other Methods Are Not Working

Congress appropriated $1.7 billion in 1986 for an assault on drugs. The result: More people buying, selling, using, and dying from drugs than ever before.

What other option would work against an evil empire that has murdered its way to ultimate power in Colombia and is bent on exporting this tyranny to the USA?

At home, many of us are already prisoners behind iron gates, afraid to attend church or allow our children to play freely.

Do the frightened and beleaguered have to move to Managua to be rescued? What better time than now for a real fight for freedom?

CONTROLLING
THE DRUG EPIDEMIC

STRONGER LAW ENFORCEMENT
IS NEEDED

Edward Koch

The Honorable Edward Koch presented the following testimony before the Select Committee on Narcotics Abuse and Control in his capacity as Mayor of New York City.

Points to Consider:

1. How many people were arrested for selling drugs in the vicinity of New York City schools? What percentage of these arrests were near elementary schools?
2. In what ways could U.S. military services and federal law enforcement agencies be used in the war against drugs?
3. Explain Mayor Koch's suggestion to realign federal law enforcement.
4. Summarize the ways in which imprisonment could be used as a deterrent.

Excerpted from testimony of Edward Koch before the House of Representatives Select Committee on Narcotics Abuse and Control, July 18, 1986.

Federal law enforcement should be realigned to meet the changing realities of drugs in America.

In 1973 America lost its first war, at a cost of more than 50,000 deaths and years of national anguish. We are now losing a second war, one that promises to exact a price far higher than Vietnam did. We are in danger of losing our greatest resource: our people.

America's Drug Problem

New York City doesn't have a drug problem: neither does Boston, Chicago, Miami, Los Angeles, Anchorage, or Honolulu have a drug problem. The *nation* has a drug problem.

America is awash with illegal narcotics. Every jurisdiction reports drug encroachment across all age, economic, ethnic, and occupational categories. The New York City police department reported more than 56,000 drug arrests in 1985, with cocaine surging in popularity. As an example, in May of 1986, cocaine arrests increased some 68 percent over May of 1985, while arrests for heroin, marijuana, and other drugs dropped five percent, 55 percent, and 46 percent respectively. . . .

Equally alarming is the presence of drugs near our schools. The Board of Education reported that during the school year just ended more than 3,500 individuals were arrested for selling drugs in the vicinity of 343 schools. Sixty-three percent of the arrests were near elementary schools. The street value of the drugs seized exceeds $1 million. Nearly half (44 percent) of the arrests were for cocaine crimes. Only three percent of those arrested were students, while 79 percent of the people arrested were over 20 years of age.

What this means is painfully clear: adult drug dealers are congregating near our schools, trying to hook our children into lives of drug dependency. This will lead to truancy, crime, and ultimately the destruction of many more young lives. . . .

Interdiction Is the Key

I firmly believe and have consistently stated that drugs are the scourge of this country. Over two years ago I laid out a plan for greater federal involvement against narcotics. I will do so again today. . . .

Interdiction is the key to stopping the supply of drugs. We must end the restrictions of the Posse Comitatus Act, which prevents use of the military in civilian law enforcement. But it is not enough to attack drugs at their source. The Army, Navy, Air Force, other military services, and federal law enforcement agencies should be deployed at our borders and on the high seas to stop the hundreds of tons of drugs that are now entering the country.

Let me cite an example of how our resources could be put to better use. The United States Navy has seven Trident nuclear submarines, each costing $1.48 billion. It is our fervent hope that none of them will ever need to be used in defense of the nation. Three months ago President Reagan declared international narcotics trafficking to be a threat to national security. If it is, shouldn't we be spending at least $3 billion, or the cost of two Trident submarines, to meet that threat? To save our people from the horror that drugs visit upon their lives and those of their families?

The Coast Guard must also be directed to quickly implement an important interdiction weapon that is not being used. In November 1984, Congress passed Public Law 99-145, the 1986 Department of Defense Appropriation Act. It provided funding for the hiring and deployment of 500 narcotics investigators for the Coast Guard, who would be deployed aboard naval vessels in drug-smuggling lanes. Last month, the Coast Guard informed me that it had not recruited or deployed even one of these investigators, but would gradually do so over the next three years.

This is scandalous! If the government is unwilling to spend the billions needed to rid us of the drug curse that assails America, shouldn't it at least spend the $15 million that Congress appropriated for these Coast Guard narcotics investigators for this fiscal year? Why is that money not being spent on this essential mission?

I pressed hard for the legislation that led to this appropriation. I frankly resent the inaction and inertia of the Coast Guard in implementing this vital interdiction asset. You should resent it also. A surgeon would not wait three years to operate on an active life-threatening cancer. Our country cannot afford the luxury of a three-year wait before effectively

Cartoon by David Seavey. Copyright 1986, *USA Today*. Reprinted with permission.

dealing with the cancer of narcotics. The Coast Guard must move now and you, the Congress, must monitor that movement!

Stronger Federal Law Enforcement Needed

Federal law enforcement should be realigned to meet the changing realities of drugs in America. The Attorney General should immediately direct at least a tripling of the number of drug enforcement agents assigned to New York and other major cities. The Federal Bureau of Investigation should devote substantial manpower against the lucrative cocaine trade. The Drug Enforcement Administration (DEA) assigns only

300 agents to the New York region, which includes New York City and several other jurisdictions. The Federal Bureau of Investigation deploys only one team of 12 agents in New York City dedicated to cocaine investigations. In 1984, the DEA Administrator said that he would need 40,000 agents worldwide to effectively curtail the drug flow into America. Two years later there are a mere 2,400 agents on the rolls.

Federal prosecution of narcotics dealers at all levels should be dramatically increased. Here in New York City the "Federal Day" program for prosecuting street-level dealers has been welcome and effective. That program should be continued here, and initiated in each federal district where conditions permit. In New York City we have exceptionally talented and committed local prosecutors who suffer from crushing caseloads. That is probably true in many other parts of the country as well. They must receive aid from the federal prosecutors. Furthermore, in order to show true federal commitment against narcotics, the United States should assume exclusive original jurisdiction over all narcotics cases in the nation for a brief and reasonable period of time.

Congress should create special United States narcotics courts to deal with the anticipated increase in federal drug prosecutions. Such courts would assure the best and most efficient processing of these cases which so directly affect life in America.

Deterrence of the drug dealer must also be a high priority in both state and federal courts. Some few jurisdictions, such as New York and Florida, provide possible life sentences for some drug crimes. The fact is, however, that few, if any, drug offenders ever serve life. Other sanctions such as harsh fines and asset forfeitures have also failed to deter such violators. The death penalty will deter them. Federal judges should have the option to sentence drug wholesalers to death. While capital punishment is an extraordinary remedy, we are facing an extraordinary peril. We must have the resolve to unequivocally signal to the drug wholesaler that the price for getting caught will be the ultimate one. For the death penalty to work, it must be used, not merely threatened.

Use Imprisonment as a Deterrent

Imprisonment is another deterrent to some. Presently the federal prison system contains some 10,000 inmates convicted of drug offenses. That number is fewer than the total narcotics inmates in the prisons of just three of our states: New York, Illinois, and Texas. The total federal prison population barely exceeds that of New York State. It is plain that the federal prison capacity must be increased.

I also recommend the designation of special federal narcotics prisons, preferably in remote locations such as the Yukon and desert areas. Segregation of drug offenders from others, and the separation from family and friends, would be additional punitive measures that could contribute to the potential for deterrence.

Moreover, the cost to the taxpayer would not be prohibitive. These prisons need not be built in dense population centers, such as New York State, where the average construction cost is $100,000 per cell. Quite the contrary. Build these prisons in the outlands, where cost is minimal and where the elements and nature provide the required security.

It is important to note that the crimes of which we speak, narcotics, involve substances not grown or produced in the United States in most instances. Cocaine, heroin, and 90 percent of the marijuana consumed here crosses international borders which the federal government is charged with policing. It is fitting, then, that the federal prisons house the persons who bring those substances into the individual states or sell them there.

We Need a Comprehensive Plan to Fight Drugs

Beyond the punitive aspect of deterrence, there is the financial, the element of profit, to be considered. It defies logic that at a time when experts estimate that some $50-75 billion in illegal drug money is generated in the United States each year we do not have a federal money-laundering statute. Congress should follow the 1984 recommendation of the President's Commission on Organized Crime and bar money transactions by those intending by these transactions to promote or profit from unlawful activity. . . .

We must not lose sight of our overriding responsibility to rid our nation of all drugs. To do this, there must be a comprehensive, consistent plan, devised and executed aggressively by the federal government, to attack the gravest threat faced by American society short of war: narcotics.

18

CONTROLLING THE DRUG EPIDEMIC

SOCIAL TRANSFORMATION IS THE ANSWER

Mimi H. Silbert

Mimi Silbert presented the following testimony before the Select Committee on Narcotics Abuse and Control in her capacity as President and Chief Executive Officer of Delancey Street Foundation, a residential treatment center for former substance abusers and ex-convicts.

Points to Consider:

1. What kind of people are at high risk for drug abuse? Why are these people at such a high risk?
2. Describe the Delancey Street Foundation. What purpose does this organization serve?
3. How does Delancey Street support itself?
4. Summarize the values that are taught and learned at Delancey Street.

Excerpted from testimony of Mimi H. Silbert before the House of Representatives Select Committee on Narcotics Abuse and Control, October 31, 1986.

While it is important to control the influx and sales of illegal drugs, we will not lick this problem until we do something about people's need for drugs.

The recent focus on drugs could shed light on a complex issue we have long ignored, or it could generate a temporary fad and hysteria which will distract us from solving the real problem at hand. Just as 30-second campaign spots cannot capture the essence of what any political leader stands for, so, too, quick media-promotable answers, a rush of insufficient, ill-directed government money, and arguments about drug testing leave unresolved the basic issue of stopping people from abusing drugs. While it is important to control the influx and sales of illegal drugs, we will *not* lick this problem until we do something about people's *need* for drugs.

People at High Risk for Drug Abuse

My twenty years of experience in this field is extensive. With doctorate degrees in Criminology and Psychology from the University of California at Berkeley, I have conducted major research and planned and evaluated projects in more than 25 cities, trained police, sheriffs, and probation officers in over 30 departments, taught college, and published many book chapters and articles. My work has been recognized by an appointment to the National Institute of Justice by President Carter, to the State Board of Corrections by Governor Deukmejian, by commendations from the State Legislature, and by San Francisco and Santa Monica Mayoral Proclamations, among others.

My experience indicates that drug abuse is highest among people who are marginal in our society. The poor, long outside the mainstream of our society, have for years been the prime candidates for substance abuse. However, as more and more groups in society become un-needed and marginal, and their values become diffused (e.g., adolescents, our workers who are facing replacement by contract labor or technology, women facing the empty nest syndrome), they become higher risk for drug abuse.

It is not enough to "just say no to drugs." We must teach people to say *yes* to life. They must feel enough involvement, commitment, opportunity, and responsibility to choose a life without drugs and without any form of self-destruction. This is not a simple task, but it is a critical one.

The Delancey Street Foundation

The organization of which I am the President and Chief Executive Officer, Delancey Street Foundation, is considered the most unique and successful residential treatment center in the country for former substance abusers and ex-convicts. Our successes have been touted by such notaries in the field as *Dr. Karl Menninger,* who states we are "the best in the world" and *Nancy Reagan* who wrote me to commend our work, along with many of the media, ranging from being featured on *This Is Your Life* to a *60 Minutes* segment, a segment of *CBS Morning News, The Today Show,* and a number of nationally circulated periodicals.

For fifteen years, Delancey Street has been rebuilding the lives of the most serious drug addicts with *no* government money. I believe it is an important model of change and provides an avenue of hope for our country.

Delancey Street currently has over 600 residents located in four facilities throughout the country: New Mexico, New York, Los Angeles, and our headquarters in San Francisco. Our population ranges in age from 12 to 68: approximately 1/4 are women, 1/3 Black, 1/3 Hispanic, and 1/3 Anglo. Despite the backgrounds of our residents, *there has never been one incident of physical violence in Delancey Street, nor has there been one arrest* in the fifteen years we've operated.

All residents, despite being functionally illiterate and unskilled when entering Delancey Street, receive a high school equivalency and are trained in three different marketable skills before graduating. Thousands of men and women have graduated into society as taxpaying citizens leading successful lives, including lawyers, realtors, sales people, the various medical professions, truck drivers, mechanics, contractors, the

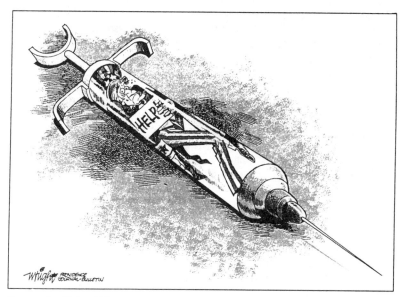

Cartoon by Richard Wright. Reprinted with permission.

prior President to the School Board, a member of the San Francisco Board of Supervisors, and even a deputy sheriff.

We have accomplished all of this, *at no cost to the taxpayer or the client.* One of the most unique features of Delancey Street is that we have never accepted any government funds, nor do we receive private operational grants. The Foundation supports itself primarily through a number of training schools which provide vocational skills to all the residents, and which also generate the Foundation's income through pooling the monies earned. These training schools include restaurant and catering, moving and trucking, terrarium and sand painting production and sales, furniture and woodwork production and sales, national specialty advertising sales to businesses and college bookstores, construction, automotive repair and antique car restoration, the operation of outdoor Christmas tree lots, and a print shop. Residents who have traditionally been unemployable welfare cases, have started, worked, and managed these training school businesses so successfully that they are the Foundation's primary source of working capital.

Changing People's Values

Aside from me, everyone working in Delancey Street is also a resident in the process of changing his or her life. There is no staff of ex-

129

perts. Instead, in Delancey Street, everyone is both a giver and a receiver. I believe we cannot do anything *to* or *for* the substance abuser. They must learn to do things *with* themselves and one another. As receivers their whole lives—receivers of welfare, of therapy, of punishment—these people must become the givers and doers. As each person learns a skill, he teaches the newer people, while learning new skills from older residents.

The treatment process is based on a return to the traditional American values. *Discipline and dignity, self respect and service, hard work and can-do attitude are key factors in the Delancey Street formula for success.* Residents work eight hours a day, are tutored until they receive a high school equivalency, attend daily classes in everything from money management to opera appreciation, attend group sessions three nights weekly, and do volunteer community work as well.

Thus, while thousands of people have succeeded in their task of no longer using drugs and no longer committing crime, we feel that our residents have succeeded in more important ways. They have pooled their resources to gain access to the same opportunities the middle and upper classes enjoy. Further, they have demanded of themselves that they make restitution to society, that they care not only about their own financial success in life, but that they care about honesty, integrity, and the values by which we remain more than a country of people living together—values which make us a society.

CONTROLLING
THE DRUG EPIDEMIC

PUNISH THE CONSUMER

William Raspberry

William Raspberry wrote the following article in his capacity as a nationally syndicated columnist for The Washington Post. *In this particular column, Mr. Raspberry argues that it is time to start targeting consumers in the war on drugs.*

Points to Consider:

1. Why is it difficult to stop drug production and drug trafficking?
2. What does the author suggest in order to eliminate drug users?
3. Do you agree with Mr. Raspberry's proposal? Why or why not?

William Raspberry, "Start Targeting Consumers in Drug War," *St. Paul Pioneer Press Dispatch,* September 9, 1987. © 1987, Washington Post Writers Group. Reprinted with permission.

Instead of chasing dealers from one floating market to the next, let's chase the customers. Arrest, prosecute, and jail them.

It is time in our war on illegal narcotics to focus on a new target: not the peasants who grow the coca plants from which the deadly cocaine is derived; not the international traffickers who process the stuff and bring it into the United States, not even the distributors and pushers who comprise the retail network.

It's time to move hard on the one crucial element in the chain: those who buy this poison.

Focus on Drug Purchasers

Tell me it isn't fair to target the user when it is the major trafficker who does the great damage, and I'll say you're correct. Tell me we shouldn't give carte blanche to the syndicates who manage the dope traffic, and you get no argument from me. I wouldn't for a minute argue that we should reduce our efforts against the drug racketeers.

But I would argue, not from fairness but from desperation, that any new effort ought to be focused on drug purchasers.

The fact is, the catalog of ways to curtail the drug traffic is distressingly short; shorter still is the list of ways that promise to be effective.

The most obvious approaches—halting production and keeping the stuff out of the country—share a near-insurmountable difficulty: the enormous profits to be had from drug trafficking.

Difficult to Combat Drug Traffickers

The money is enough to subvert weak governments, and enough to finance criminal armies to combat the anti-drug efforts of stronger ones. Enough officials in the first category have been bought, and enough in the second have been killed or intimidated into inaction, that there is little hope of a successful effort to halt production.

In addition, given the porousness of this country's borders and the drug traffickers resources—diplomatic pouches, innocent-appearing individual smugglers, and private (and disposable) planes and boats—it's hard to imagine a successful campaign to keep the lucrative drugs out of the country. And once they are here, the openness of travel in this country reduces their distribution to virtual child's play.

How much does it take to overwhelm or corrupt an undermanned sheriff's department in a sparsely populated Florida county? How hard is it to persuade an already-intimidated deputy to find a way to occupy himself somewhere else at 9 o'clock tomorrow night?

What disruptions to ordinary vehicular traffic would it take to interdict the flow of narcotics along, say, Interstate 95, through Florida, Georgia, the Carolinas, Washington, D.C., Pennsylvania, New Jersey, and New York? It's easy to be misled by reports of huge narcotics "busts" along this eastern artery into supposing that we are seriously interrupting the traffic. The real story is not in those few well-publicized busts but in the common knowledge that the drug dealing in our neighborhoods continues unabated.

Time to Target Customers

It's time to try a new direction. It's time to look at drug users, not as "victims" or as relatively minor players in the drug scene but as the one indispensable element in the drama. Retire the users, and you close down the play.

And how do you do that? By targeting the customers of the open-air drug markets that have turned struggling neighborhoods into war zones. The dealers don't worry about an arrest or a confiscation in the unlikely event they get caught before they melt into the background. It's just another cost of doing their incredibly lucrative business. But the user is another matter. The drug customer, whether a college student, a young professional, a wage-earner or a suburban sophisticate, can't melt.

And he can't afford the consequences of getting caught. There is, for him, no profit in the drug market to offset the damage to his reputation or the loss of his (or his parents') car. He has only the prospect of a few minutes' pleasure to balance against the risks of arrest.

Mr. Cool

Cartoon by David Seavey. Copyright 1986, *USA Today.* Reprinted with permission.

Arrest, Prosecute, and Jail Them

I say it's time to increase the risks. Instead of chasing dealers from one floating market to the next, let's chase the customers. Arrest, prosecute, and jail them. The law says we can take their cars. So let's take them—routinely. If you want to leave an opening so that an innocent owner can reclaim the automobile he swears he didn't know was being used for drug procurement, that's OK by me. Once.

But the second time Mr. Innocent's car is used to fetch drugs, send it to the auction yard. My guess is that there won't be many second times.

Of course it isn't fair to move more harshly against the occasional user than against the professional who makes his living dealing drugs.

But how fair is it to the residents of the neighborhoods to let their children's playgrounds be turned into drug markets? Many of these residents are trying desperately, and with dismaying lack of success, to reclaim their communities and save their children.

It is they, and not the out-of-the-neighborhood thrill-seekers, who deserve our sympathy and our help.

And the best way to help these innocent victims of the drug traffic, and perhaps to make a serious dent in the traffic as well, is to take away the one indispensable participant: the customer.

20

CONTROLLING
THE DRUG EPIDEMIC

EDUCATE THE USER

Denis Wadley

Denis Wadley wrote the following article in his capacity as a Minneapolis teacher and Vice President of Americans for Democratic Action. His story appeared in the Minneapolis Star Tribune.

Points to Consider:

1. Why does the author compare the war on drugs to the McCarthy era?
2. How does Congress want to deal with the drug problem? How does the author suggest we approach the drug problem?
3. Describe what happened when an experiment was run to get students to avoid or stop smoking cigarettes. What were the results of this experiment?
4. Why does the author believe the war on drugs is misguided?

Denis Wadley, "The Misguided War on Drugs," *Minneapolis Star Tribune,* September 18, 1986. Reprinted by permission of the *Star Tribune, Newspaper of the Twin Cities.*

Drug education has been drastically underfunded for years, largely in misguided efforts by the Reagan administration to save money.

If anyone wants to know where the liberals are these days, Congress isn't the place to look; and if one wants an issue that distinguishes liberals from conservatives, the drug issue isn't one. On that issue the House of Representatives, the last bastion of resistance to the Reagan Revolution, is trying a right-end run around the administration.

Drugs Are the Enemy

You have to read the news twice to believe it, but the Democratic-controlled House has passed a bill that revives the terrible old days of Pat McCarran and Joe McCarthy and turns civil liberties on its head. This time communism isn't the enemy; it's cocaine, marijuana, and heroin.

For years politicians have called for a war on drugs. The president did, too, right after his 1980 election. He was willing to do anything but spend money on it. So we had speeches, pamphlets, dedicated committees, moral indignation, and a steady increase in drug use.

Nancy Reagan's many appearances and exhortations have no doubt been helpful, but they've been about the only thing the administration has done that has made any impression at all.

She has the right idea. The House has the wrong one.

Meaningless Talk in Congress

The House bill targets the drug dealers and the smugglers who bring the stuff into the country (from Latin America particularly) and the farmers who grow the stuff there and make a living at it.

The bill proposes two intolerable measures that show how shallow a commitment to civil liberties many politicians have. They want capital punishment for drug dealers and use of the military to enforce drug laws. Even the administration doesn't advocate these things.

It's the same old meaningless talk the crime-war demagogues use in every election year. Fight crime by increasing penalties and decreasing rights. These are usually the politicians who want "to get government off the back of the individual."

Right now the only federal capital crime is murder of a public official—and very few officials are covered. One doesn't even get the death sentence for treason or sabotage. But they want it for drug dealing.

In no other area of civilian law is the military permitted to enforce law or make arrests. But these people—most of them Democrats—want it for drug dealers.

> ## "JUST SAY NO"
>
> *The hope for ridding society of the drug scourge is education and treatment, especially the former. Nancy Reagan's "just say no" may be over-simplified and too little, but it aims in the right direction.*
>
> *We reduced tobacco smoking by one-third with sustained education. We've even begun to cut consumption of booze by convincing people drunks are less cool than Hollywood used to think.*
>
> *We can do the same with drugs. Indeed, with the exception of crack, usage has come down in recent years, most noticeably and beneficially among the young.*
>
> Jim Fain, "Political Prattle on Drugs Ignores a Sure Antidote," Star Tribune, *June 1, 1988*

Can We Patrol Drug Use?

Crimes involving illegal pleasures will survive, one way or another, wherever there is a market. Prohibition taught us that with a vengeance. Would *that* problem have been solved by making bootlegging a capital crime? Would the army have done better than the FBI in enforcing those laws?

Should we perhaps try to curb tobacco smoking by arresting the growers?

An example is illustrative: Ten years ago an experiment was run to test the most effective way to get students in secondary schools to avoid or stop smoking cigarettes. In one school stiff rules were set down, with inflexible penalties like fines, suspensions, and expulsions. In another there were exhortations, moral and medical, with heavy advertising. In a third, doctors came in, gave basic medical facts with X-ray illustrations and dry statistics, and left printed information. Later surveys showed that the first method promoted more secret smoking, not less; the second had a small effect; but the third prompted measurable decrease.

Nothing really worked well. But one thing did work a bit; persuasion. Ordinarily that word rings weak, like passing a resolution while the city is burning. But if a person is convinced of harmful effects, he patrols himself. If not, often many others cannot patrol him.

Cartoon by David Seavey. Copyright 1986, *USA Today.* Reprinted with permission.

We Need Drug Education

Drug education has been drastically underfunded for years, largely in misguided efforts by the Reagan administration to save money. Draconian measures now won't make up for that; they simply create new problems in other areas.

Moreover, if drug enforcement should succeed in cutting off one route for drugs into this country, does anyone doubt another will open up just as fast, as long as there is a market?

The enemy is us. The public, so tolerant of drugs in fact, while so hostile in rhetoric, is the reason this trade flourishes. In this matter the victim is also the villain, for almost all use is voluntary, even at first with addicting drugs. Cut the demand, and we cut the supply. Political people often see all reform as a matter of rewards and punishments; where have these gotten us thus far? More progress has been made in reducing smoking than in eliminating drugs, and cigarettes are legal.

Congress should consort less with the military and more with the schools on these matters; it should propose to cut off demand rather than lives. Reagan is fond of saying the government can't do everything for us. The House bill tried. It is fundamentally misguided.

21

CONTROLLING
THE DRUG EPIDEMIC

LEGALIZING DRUGS:
POINTS AND COUNTERPOINTS

USA Today vs. Patrick Cox

The following counterpoints were excerpted from the opinion page of
USA Today, *a national daily newspaper. The point is the opinion of*
USA Today; *Patrick Cox wrote the counterpoint in his capacity as a*
political and economic analyst and freelance writer.

Points to Consider:

1. What kind of arguments are advanced to support the legalization of drugs?
2. Why do the authors of the point disagree with legalization?
3. How have drugs contributed to the violence in our cities?
4. Do you agree with the point or counterpoint? Why?

THE POINT—by *USA Today*

Baltimore Mayor Kurt Schmoke thinks it's time to start talking about legalizing drugs.

So do mayors in Oakland, Calif.; Charles Town, W.Va.; Minneapolis, Minn.; and Washington, D.C.

William F. Buckley, the conservative editor and columnist, doesn't think talk is enough. He wants to legalize drugs now. So does at least one New York state senator, who has introduced a bill to do exactly that.

A California think tank says it's getting a call a week from members of Congress asking about the issue.

A Frustrated Nation

It seems that as the nation grows frustrated with its dope problem, the ideas for solving it get dopier.

The latest idea is to just give up—or at least to study whether giving up is a good idea.

The thinking goes like this:

We can't win the drug war because we're hopelessly outgunned, so we should make drugs legal. That will drive down prices, push pushers out of business, and cut crime. It will save billions wasted on law enforcement and free up money for anti-drug education.

You can read that view elsewhere. It's simple, clear, and superficially appealing.

It's also dead wrong.

Legalization Is Surrender

Legalization is no solution. It's surrender. The arguments for it won't stand close scrutiny.

► Sure, making drugs legal will drive down prices. If drugs are cheap enough, and easy enough to get, pushers will indeed be pushed out of business.

But if drugs are cheap, more people will use them.

That's no solution.

► Sure, legalization would cut down some crime—the violent, drug-smuggling variety you see on *Miami Vice*.

But would it eliminate the robberies, muggings, and burglaries committed by junkies who would still need to feed their habits, even at lower prices? No.

And how about violent, irrational crimes committed by people high on drugs like PCP and cocaine? They'd climb.

That's no solution.

►Sure, we could save money on law enforcement—$8 billion a year, according to one estimate.

LEGALIZERS MINIMIZE THE PROBLEM

Legalizers minimize the catastrophic effect that legalization will have on public health, an effect that will far outweigh the savings in law enforcement. We had an inkling of that during Prohibition. Prohibition was a law-enforcement catastrophe but, during its early years at least, a public-health triumph. The rates of such alcohol-related illnesses as cirrhosis of the liver and alcoholic psychosis went down remarkably.

Well, you ask, if alcohol is now legal, what is the logic of prohibiting cocaine and heroin? No logic, just history. Alcohol use is so ancient and so universal a practice that it cannot be repealed. The question is not: Which is worse, alcohol or cocaine? The question is: Which is worse, alcohol alone or alcohol plus coke and heroin and PCP? Alcohol is here to stay. To legalize other drugs is to declare that the rest of the pharmacy is here to stay, too.

Charles Krauthammer, "Legalizing Drugs: Only a Quick Fix," Star Tribune, May 22, 1988

But we'd lose more. A 1983 study found that drug abuse cost the nation $60 billion in one year for lost productivity, medical costs, drug-related crime, and the like.

That's no solution, either.

Keep Up the Fight

Legalization deserves to be debated, as does almost any idea for solving the nation's most frustrating problem.

But it is not an idea whose time has come.

Until a new approach proves its merit, the drug war must be waged with conventional weapons—education, rehabilitation, and aggressive law enforcement.

That may not yield quick results. It may not ease the frustration in Baltimore, Oakland, Charles Town, Minneapolis, Washington, or a thousand other communities.

But it will mean we're fighting drugs. And fighting, not quitting, offers our only hope for winning the war on drugs.

Cartoon by David Seavey. Copyright 1988, *USA Today*. Reprinted with permission.

THE COUNTERPOINT—by Patrick Cox

Every time you walk outside, you're twice as likely to be mugged, injured, or killed because addicts pay a 10,000 percent markup on the drugs they need to satisfy their dependencies.

Even when you and those you love are locked in your homes at night, you're twice as likely to be burgled, injured, or killed because drugs are treated as a criminal problem instead of a medical one.

This is the price we all pay for the crusade against intoxicants. But some pay more.

Drugs and Violence

Those who ride in chauffeured limos between the halls of Congress and high-security neighborhoods are the last to feel the violence that prohibition has created. The families and cops who live and work in low-income areas, however, know it too well.

Some say it's something of a miracle that politicians have begun to openly doubt the "war on drugs." But the real miracle is that so few voices have been raised so timidly after so long.

Scientists have been telling us that drug prohibitions are the cause of most violent crimes, gang warfare, and police deaths since drugs were banned. The notion that now we have to gather more evidence is absurd. I could fill this page with scholarly footnotes, but it's unlikely it would have any impact on those who endorse drug prohibitions without any evidential basis. Nevertheless, I will mention a few of the scholars whose work should be heeded:

► Lester Grinspoon of Harvard Medical School.

► Thomas Szasz, State University of New York Medical School at Syracuse.

► Arnold Trebach, The American University, who wrote *The Great Drug War.*

► Ronald Hamowy, University of Alberta, who edited *Dealing with Drugs.*

► Steven Wizotsky, University of Wisconsin, who wrote *Breaking the Impasse on the War on Drugs.*

I would also cite Milton Friedman and William F. Buckley Jr. for their remarkably cogent analyses of original research.

Make Drugs Legal

We have two choices: One is to continue on the present course toward a police state, using the imaginary threat of a totally addicted and fractured society to create crime while increasing taxes to fight it. The other is to substitute compassion and scholarship for fear and stupidity, decriminalizing drugs so that we can live in relative peace and security.

The high price of illegal drugs is paid not only by the addicts who would be allowed to buy clean, inexpensive, and less injurious substitutes in a better world. We all pay—in lives, money, and freedom. And we are exporting the madness, propagating poverty and hatred of the USA among innocent citizens in Panama and other Third World nations. Every day that passes is another day we simply cannot afford.

WHAT IS EDITORIAL BIAS?

This activity may be used as an individualized study guide for students in libraries and resource centers or as a discussion catalyst in small group and classroom discussions.

The capacity to recognize an author's point of view is an essential reading skill. The skill to read with insight and understanding involves the ability to detect different kinds of opinions or bias. Sex bias, race bias, ethnocentric bias, political bias, and religious bias are five basic kinds of opinions expressed in editorials and all literature that attempts to persuade. They are briefly defined below.

Five Kinds of Editorial Opinion or Bias

SEX BIAS—The expression of dislike for and/or feeling of superiority over the opposite sex or a particular sexual minority

RACE BIAS—The expression of dislike for and/or feeling of superiority over a racial group

ETHNOCENTRIC BIAS—The expression of a belief that one's own group, race, religion, culture, or nation is superior. Ethnocentric persons judge others by their own standards and values

POLITICAL BIAS—The expression of political opinions and attitudes about domestic or foreign affairs

RELIGIOUS BIAS—The expression of a religious belief or attitude

---

Guidelines

1. From the readings in Chapter Four, locate five sentences that provide examples of editorial opinion or bias.

2. Write down each of the above sentences and determine what kind of bias each sentence represents. Is it **sex bias, race bias, ethnocentric bias, political bias** or **religious bias?**

3. Make up one sentence statements that would be an example of each of the following: **sex bias, race bias, ethnocentric bias, political bias** and **religious bias.**

4. See if you can locate five sentences that are **factual** statements from the readings in Chapter Four.

APPENDIX

Selected General Accounting Office (GAO) Reports and Testimonies on Federal Drug Control Efforts

This appendix presents selected GAO reports and testimonies since fiscal year 1980 related to federal drug control efforts. Requests for copies of GAO publications should be sent to: U.S. General Accounting Office, P.O. Box 6015, Gaithersburg, Maryland 20877—telephone (202) 275-6241.

Coordination, Oversight, and Policy

National Drug Policy Board: Leadership Evolving, Greater Role in Developing Budgets Possible. GAO/GGD-88-24, 2/12/88.

The Need for Strong Central Oversight of the Federal Government's War on Drugs. Testimony before the House Select Committee on Narcotics Abuse and Control, Senate Committee on the Judiciary. GAO/T-GGD-87-17, 5/14/87.

Reported Federal Drug Abuse Expenditures—Fiscal Years 1981 to 1985. GAO/GGD-85-61, 6/3/85.

Interdepartmental Cooperation of Drug Enforcement Programs. Testimony before the House Committee on Government Operations: Government Information, Justice and Agriculture Subcommittee. 2/25/83.

Drug Enforcement Coordination. Testimony before the House Committee on the Judiciary: Crime Subcommittee. 2/17/83.

FBI-DEA Task Forces: An Unsuccessful Attempt at Joint Operations. GAO/GGD-82-50, 3/26/82.

Narcotics Enforcement Policy. Testimony before the House Committee on the Judiciary: Crime Subcommittee. 12/10/81.

Changes Needed to Strengthen Federal Efforts to Combat Narcotics Trafficking. Testimony before the Senate Committee on Appropriations: Treasury, Postal Service and General Government Subcommittee. 4/22/80.

Drug Abuse Problem in the Southwest. Testimony before the Senate Committee on Appropriations: Commerce, Justice, State, the Judiciary and Related Agencies Subcommittee. 4/14/80.

Federal Drug Enforcement and Supply Control Efforts. Testimony before the House Committee on Energy and Commerce: Commerce, Transportation and Tourism Subcommittee. 3/10/80.

Gains Made in Controlling Illegal Drugs, Yet the Drug Trade Flourishes. GAO/GGD-80-4, 10/25/79.

Financial Tools and Assets Forfeiture

Internal Controls: Drug Enforcement Administration's Use of Forfeited Personal Property. GAO/GGD-87-20, 12/10/86.

Bank Secrecy Act: Treasury Can Improve Implementation of the Act. GAO/GGD-86-95, 6/11/86.

Better Care and Disposal of Seized Cars, Boats and Planes Should Save Money and Benefit Law Enforcement. GAO/PLRD-83-94, 7/15/83.

Asset Forfeiture—A Seldom Used Tool in Combating Drug Trafficking. GAO/GGD-81-51, 4/10/81.

Implementation of Bank Secrecy Act's Reporting Requirements. Testimony before the House Committee on Banking, Finance and Urban Affairs: General Oversight and Investigations Subcommittee. 10/1/80.

Taking the Profit Out of Crime. Testimony before the Senate Committee on the Judiciary: Criminal Justice Subcommittee. 7/23/80.

Interdiction

Drug Smuggling: Large Amounts of Illegal Drugs Not Seized by Federal Authorities. GAO/GGD-87-91, 6/12/87.

Federal Drug Interdiction Efforts. Testimony before the House Committee on Government Operations: Government Information, Justice and Agriculture Subcommittee, 9/9/86.

Coordination of Federal Drug Interdiction Efforts. GAO/GGD-85-67, 7/15/85.

The Role of the National Narcotics Border Interdiction System in Coordinating Federal Drug Interdiction Efforts. Testimony before the House Committee on Government Operations: Government Information, Justice and Agriculture Subcommittee. 3/21/84.

The Need for Improved Intelligence Capabilities to Support Drug Interdiction Programs. Testimony before the House Committee on Government Operations: Government Information, Justice and Agriculture Subcommittee. 7/7/83.

Federal Drug Interdiction Efforts Need Strong Central Oversight. GAO/GGD-83-52, 6/13/83.

Coast Guard Drug Interdiction on the Texas Coast. GAO/CED-81-104, 5/19/81.

International Drug Control

Drug Control: River Patrol Craft for the Government of Bolivia. GAO/NSIAD-88-10IFS, 2/2/88.

Drug Control: U.S.-Mexico Opium Poppy and Marijuana Aerial Eradication Program. GAO/NSIAD-88-73, 1/11/88.

U.S.-Mexico Opium Poppy and Marijuana Aerial Eradication Program. Testimony before the House Select Committee on Narcotics Abuse and Control. GAO/T-NSIAD-87-42, 8/5/87.

Status Report on GAO Review of the U.S. International Narcotics Control Program. Testimony before the House Committee on Foreign Affairs: Special International Narcotics Control Subcommittee. GAO/T-NSIAD-87-40, 7/29/87.

Drug Control: International Narcotics Control Activities of the United States. GAO/NSIAD-87-72BR, 1/30/87.

Suggested Improvements in Management of International Narcotics Control Program. GAO/ID-81-13, 11/13/80.

Investigations

Drug Investigations: Organized Crime Drug Enforcement Task Force Program's Accomplishments. GAO/GGD-87-64BR, 5/6/87.

Drug Investigations: Organized Crime Drug Enforcement Task Force Program: A Coordinating Mechanism. GAO/GGD-86-73BR, 7/17/86.

Customs Service's Participation in Follow-Up Investigations of Drug Smuggling Interdictions in South Florida. GAO/GGD-84-37, 7/18/84.

Investigations of Major Drug Trafficking Organizations. GAO/GGD-84-36, 3/5/84.

Organized Crime Drug Enforcement Task Forces: Status and Observation. GAO/GGD-84-35, 12/9/83.

Stronger Crackdown Needed on Clandestine Laboratories Manufacturing Dangerous Drugs. GAO/GGD-82-6, 11/6/81.

The Drug Enforcement Administration's CENTAC Program—An Effective Approach to Investigating Major Traffickers that Needs to Be Expanded. GAO/GGD-80-52, 3/27/80.

Military Role

Drug Law Enforcement: Military Assistance for Anti-Drug Agencies. GAO/GGD-88-27, 12/23/87.

Coordination of Requests for Military Assistance to Civilian Law Enforcement Agencies. GAO/GGD-84-27, 11/2/83.

Military Cooperation with Civilian Law Enforcement Agencies. Testimony before the House Committee on the Judiciary: Crime Subcommittee. 7/28/83.

BIBLIOGRAPHY I

Narcotics Trafficking and
U.S. Law Enforcement Policies

These publications may be available at a nearby public or research library.

Bakalar, James B. Grinspoon, Lester.
Drug Control in a Free Society. New York, Cambridge University Press, 1984. 174 p.

Brinkley, Joel.
A World of Drugs: America as Target. New York Times, Sept. 9, 1984, p. 1, 12; Sept. 10, p. A1, A12; Sept. 11, p. A1, A16; Sept. 12, p. A1, A16; Sept. 13, p. A1, A16-A17; Sept. 14, p. A1, A12.
Series on U.S. international enforcement efforts emphasizes official strategy, support for suspending foreign aid to drug-producing nations, and imposing trade sanctions and reducing military assistance to drug-producers.

Carpenter, Ted Galen.
The U.S. Campaign Against International Narcotics Trafficking: A Cure Worse Than the Disease. Washington, Cato Institute, 1985. 23 p. (Policy Analysis No. 63)
Finds that the Reagan administration's campaign to destroy global narcotics trafficking "is futile and counterproductive. . .and seriously complicates—and compromises—U.S. foreign policy."

Drugs and American Society, edited by Robert Emmet Long. New York, Wilson, 1986. 206 p.
This collection of reprinted articles discusses both trafficking and abuse.

Fisher, Kevin.
Trends in Extraterritorial Narcotics Control: Slamming the Stable Door after the Horse Has Bolted. Journal of International Law and Politics, v. 16, Winter 1984: 353-413.

Harding, Jeffrey Lee.
International Narcotics Control: A Proposal to Eradicate an International Menace. California Western International Law Journal, v. 14, Summer 1984: 530-554.

Lieber, James.
Coping with Cocaine. Atlantic Monthly, v. 257, Jan. 1986: 39-48.
Raises questions about U.S. enforcement policies which stress interdiction and eradication at the source.

McBee, Susanna.
Flood of Drugs—A Losing Battle. U.S. News and World Report, v. 98, Mar. 25, 1985: 52-57.
Contends that "corruption, global politics and nature conspire to hamper the drive to cut off the flow of narcotics at the source."

Reuter, Peter.
The (continued) Vitality of Mythical Numbers. Public Interest, No. 75, Spring 1984: 135-147.
Charges that statistics on narcotics addicts and narcotic-related crimes are a mythical "routine product of government agencies."

————

Eternal Hope: America's Quest for Narcotics Control. Public Interest, No. 79, Spring 1985: 79-95.
Explores reasons for "failures" of U.S. foreign production control efforts to reduce illegal drug availability in the U.S. in the long-term. Suggests greater focus on drug distribution systems and continuation of efforts to reduce production for possible short-term benefits, once the limitations of production control policies are acknowledged.

Weissman, J. C.
Drug Offense Sentencing Practices in the United States of America. Bulletin on Narcotics, v. 36, July-Sept. 1984: 27-41.

Wendland, Michael. Wilkinson, Barbara
Doctors Who Deal. Monthly Detroit, v. 9, Feb. 1985: 55-61.
Describes the illegal diversion of prescription medicines and controlled substances by unethical physicians and the reluctance of pharmaceutical companies to impose voluntary limits on problem pills.

U.S. Congress. House. Committee on Foreign Affairs.
U.S. International Narcotics Control Programs. Hearing, 99th Congress, 1st session. Mar. 19, 1985. Washington, G.P.O., 1985. 139 p.

U.S. Congress. House. Committee on the Judiciary.
Subcommittee on Crime. Diversion of Prescription Drugs to Illegal
Channels and Dangerous Drug Diversion Control Act. Hearings, 98th
Congress, lst and 2nd sessions, on H.R. 4698. Washington, G.P.O.,
1985. 466 p. Hearings held June 29, 1983 and Feb. 22, 1984. "Serial
no. 139"

U.S. Congress. House.
Select Committee on Narcotics Abuse and Control. Annual Report
for the Year 1984 of the Select Committee on Narcotics Abuse and
Control, 98th Congress, 2nd session, together with additional views.
Washington, G.P.O., 1985. 211 p. "SCNAC-98-2-11"

———————

Issues Affecting Federal, State, and Local Efforts to Combat Drug Trafficking and Drug Abuse; Report. Washington, G.P.O., 1985. 75 p. At
head of title: 98th Congress, 2nd session, House, committee print.
"SCNAC-98-2-9"

U.S. Congress. Senate. Committee on Appropriations.
Subcommittee on Defense. Department of Defense. Support for Drug
Interdiction. Hearing 98th Congress, 2nd session. Nov. 14, 1984.
Washington, G.P.O., 1985. 43 p. (Hearing, Senate, 98th Congress,
2nd session, S. Hrg. 98-1285)

U.S. Congress. Senate.
Committee on Banking, Housing, and Urban Affairs. Drug Money
Laundering. Hearing, 99th Congress, lst session, on S. 571. Jan. 25,
1985. Washington, G.P.O., 1985. 144 p. (Hearing, Senate, 99th Congress, lst session. S. Hrg. 99-8)

U.S. Office of the Attorney General
Annual Report of the Organized Crime Drug Enforcement Task Force
Program. Washington, Department of Justice, 1985. 130 p.

U.S. President's Commission on Organized Crime.
America's Habit: Drug Abuse, Drug Trafficking, and Organized Crime:
Report to the President and the Attorney General. Washington, The
Commission, 1986. 454 p.

BIBLIOGRAPHY II

Narcotics Interdiction

This bibliography presents literature on the topic of controlling narcotics traffic. It also discusses military assistance efforts, congressional action on the topic, and other related issues.

The border war on drugs.
Washington, Office of Technology Assessment, for sale by the Supt. of Docs., G.P.O., 1987. 62 p. LRS87-2925
"Characterizes the drug smuggling problem and the interdiction efforts now in place within the responsible federal agencies. Describes technologies in use, under development, and potentially available for countering smuggling by the various modes—private modes—private vessels, private aircraft, land vehicles, commercial carriers, and through official ports of entry."

Byrd, Lee.
Should soldiers become drug policy? Philadelphia Inquirer, July 18, 1986: 1. Newsp.
"U.S. military commanders have long agreed with civil libertarians that soldiers should not be in the business of hunting down criminal suspects, at home or abroad. But Congress and the Administration increasingly have made an exception of the illicit drug trade."

Controversy over omnibus drug legislation: pros & cons.
Congressional Digest, v. 65, Nov. 1986: whole issue (257-288 p.) LRS86-10108
Included in this report is a discussion on whether or not the U.S. armed forces should "play a major role in interdicting drug traffic into the United States."

Douglass, Joseph E., Jr. Sejna, Jan.
Drugs, narcotics, and national security. Global Affairs, v. 2, Fall 1987: 67-85. LRS87-8732
"The use of drugs and narcotics as a political weapon targeted directly against the United States and as a direct threat to U.S. national security is still not recognized. . . .That there exists a major national security problem linked to illicit drug and narcotics trafficking is, however, patently obvious. . . .To understand the broad nature of the national security problem, the strategies and action of the two Com-

munist giants, China and the Soviet Union, are examined in this paper. Particular attention is placed on operation Druzba Narodov. This material...shows how U.S. national security is deliberately affected."

Ehrenfeld, Rachel.
Narco-terrorism: The Kremlin connection. Washington, Heritage Foundation. 1987. 6 p. (Heritage Lectures no. 89) LRS87-7698
"Today, countries controlled, influenced, and supported by the Soviet Union are playing an important part in trafficking drugs into the United States, to wit Cuba, Bulgaria, Syria, and Nicaragua. Growing evidence is coming to light about the connection between these countries and the training, funding, and arming of terrorist organizations as well as trafficking drugs into the United States and other Western countries."

Halloran, Richard.
Pentagon says drug war will cost $2 billion. New York Times, May 17, 1988: A17. LRS88-3638
"The Defense Department has begun gearing up for an expanded role in the war on drugs, and senior Pentagon officials have warned Congress that the effort will cost $2 billion. The officials said that if Congress did not appropriate the extra money, United States military operations would have to be reduced."

Koch, Edward I.
A war on drugs? Use the armed forces. Washington Post, June 20, 1985: A21. LRS85-15835
New York Mayor argues that "the United States remains under siege, confronted by a tidal wave of drugs. Let's use the weapons at hand. Let's commit the military to the defense of the nation by deploying our Armed Forces along our borders and on the high seas to interdict drugs."

Korb, Lawrence J.
DOD assistance in the war on drugs. Police Chief, v. 52, Oct. 1985: 57-58, 60-62. LRS85-9386
Concludes that "law enforcement faces formidable obstacles in winning the battle against drug traffickers. The enemy is strong and getting stronger. But the Department of Defense has an appreciation of policing efforts and is committed to assisting these efforts within the constraints of the law." Other aspects of the war on drugs are considered in the Oct. 1985 issue of Police Chief.

Kristol, Irving.
War on drugs? then get serious and use the military. Washington Post, Mar. 28, 1988: A15. LRS88-2736

Argues that "the United States has a material incentive as well as moral motive to stop the commerce in drugs across its borders. We have the moral authority to designate it as piracy, and we have the power to act on this designation. If we are at all serious about a 'war on drugs,' let's begin by taking appropriate military action."

Marshall, Jonathan.
Drugs and United States foreign policy. In Dealing with Drugs: Consequences of Government Control, edited by Ronald Hamowy. Lexington, Lexington Books (D.C. Health and Company), 1987. p. 137-176. HV5825.D38 1987

"Almost invariably federal officials adopt military metaphors to describe their ceaseless efforts to combat . . . [the international drug] trade. Yet just as war is the continuation of politics by other means, so the 'war on drugs' has become an extension of foreign policy by other means."

Meese, Edwin, III.
Another option in the fight against drugs. Washington Post, Aug. 4, 1986: A13. LRS86-14499

U.S. Attorney General responds to discussions of Operation Blast Furnace in Bolivia and comments on the use of the U.S. military in drug enforcement.

Moore, Molly.
Pentagon almost a bust in drug war; cost of success last year moves GAO to ambiguous conclusions. Washington Post, June 3, 1988: A17.

Moore, Richter H., Jr.
Posse Comitatus revisited: the use of the military in civil law enforcement. Journal of Criminal Justice, v. 15, no. 5, 1987: 375-386. LRS87-11313

"The growing drug problem in the United States and the inability of federal and local law enforcement officials to meet the challenge of massive drug inflow led Congress in 1981 to enact legislation providing for military cooperation with civilian law enforcement officials. Although recognizing the Posse Comitatus Act restrictions, the law opens the door for extensive use of the military in civilian law enforcement."

Morrison, David C.

The Pentagon's drug wars. National Journal, v. 18, Sept. 6, 1986: 2104-2109. LRS86-7710

"The Defense Department's expanding role in the war on drugs poses questions of civil liberties as well as whether the new mission helps or hurts military readiness."

Nadelmann, Ethan A.

U.S. drug policy: a bad export. Foreign Policy, no. 70, Spring 1988: 83-108. LRS88-2366

Criticizes current U.S. efforts to curb Latin American drug trafficking and national drug use. "There is good reason to believe that the current American approach actually may be exacerbating most aspects of what is commonly identified as the drug problem." Author considers possible methods for improving drug policy.

Rasky, Susan F.

Senate factions search for way to widen military role on drugs. New York Times, May 13, 1988: A1, A15. LRS88-3705

"The drive to expand the Pentagon's anti-drug functions reflected growing election-year pressure on Congress to have the armed forces act against a flow of narcotics into the country that civilian law enforcement has been unable to stem."

Reuter, Peter. Crawford, Gordon. Dave, Jonathan.

Sealing the borders: the effects of increased military participation in drug interdiction. Santa Monica, Calif. Rand, 1988. 155 p.

"R-3594-USDP"

"Rising concern with drug use in the United States has led to increased emphasis on the interdiction of drugs before they reach this country. The military services are now being asked to assume a substantial share of the burden of this interdiction. In light of this development, the office of the Under Secretary of Defense for Policy requested that RAND carry out an analysis of the consequences of further increases in the military involvement in drug interdiction efforts, focusing particularly on how this might influence the consumption of cocaine and marijuana."

Rice, Paul Jackson.

New laws and insights encircle the Posse Comitatus Act. Military Law Review, v. 104, Spring 1984: 109-138.

"In 1981, Congress passed an act entitled, 'Military Cooperation with Civilian Law Enforcement Officials.' Through this new law, Congress attempted to clarify and modify the Posse Comitatus Act. It clarified the law in the areas of providing criminal information, military equipment and facilities, military personnel to train civilian law enforcement personnel, and expert military advisors to the civilian law enforcement community. Congress modified the Posse Comitatus Act so that military personnel may operate military equipment in assisting civilian law enforcement personnel. This assistance is quite limited. Under implementing Department of Defense guidance, the Navy and Marine Corps may exercise aggressive assistance to civilian law enforcement officials. Certain issues, such as the military undercover agent and the joint military-civilian patrol, were not affected by the 1981 legislation. They remain in sensitive areas in the day to day interface between military and civilian police. Reimbursement to the Department of Defense for services provided remains a key issue in implementing the 1981 Act."

Sciolino, Elaine.
Narcotics and foreign policy: diplomats do not hurry to enlist in the war on drugs. New York Times, Feb. 21, 1988: A3. LRS88-861
Contends that "part of the reason for the lack of concerted action is that drug trafficking has in recent years been treated more as a domestic scourge than as a foreign policy concern. In fact, for many officials, the drug issue is little more than an irritant that gets in the way of diplomacy."

Walker, William O., III.
Drug control and national security. Diplomatic History, v. 12, Spring 1988: 187-199. LRS88-3114
The article looks at the role of drugs in U.S. foreign policy. "Contemporary anti-drug foreign policy has important historical precedents. An explication of current policy and its historical antecedents. . . may lead to more appropriate responses to what is undeniably a serious national problem."

Weinberger, Caspar W.
Our troops shouldn't be drug cops: don't draft the military to solve a law-enforcement problem. Washington Post, May 11, 1988: C2. LRS88-3706
Former Secretary of Defense argues that "calling for the use of the government's full military resources to put a stop to the drug trade makes for hot and exciting rhetoric. But responding to those calls, as Congress is on the verge of doing, would make for terrible nation-security policy, poor politics, and guaranteed failure in the campaign against drugs."

Wilson, George C. Moore, Molly.
Pentagon warns of a no-win mission: military says offensive against drugs would overstretch resources. Washington Post, May 13, 1988: A4.

Reports that "the Defense Department. . .agreed with members of Congress that the armed forces could do more to combat drugs, but warned that the effort would take billions of dollars, divert troops and weapons from their primary missions, and drugs would still flow into the United States."